P

MW01289777

Pastor Jacob Rodriguez has carefully and creatively outlined the "shifts" that must take place if we are going to deepen our relationship with God, find solutions to life's difficult dilemmas, and become what God has created us to be. *Shift* is an invitation to experience God's best for your life.

Anthony Romo, Evangelist and Assistant Pastor, Phoenix First Apostolic Church, Phoenix, AZ

This book is a fresh look at a problem that consumes youth in every generation. As we grow, we are constantly challenged to push against the odds and not be taken by the currents. *Shift* addresses the elephant in the room. It not only addresses the issue, but provides tools to shift and make a change. This book is very well balanced with the real issues of today and gives real answers. It could not have come at a better time. I hope you enjoy this book as much as I have. This book will inspire you; it will cause you to reflect. But most of all, this book will challenge you to *Shift!*

Omar Cortez, President, National Messengers of Peace

Shift really does provide a true resource to shift something in your life. Using the three shift methods (Upward, Inward, Forward) it'll guide you through an open and honest conversation in regards to your faith or even your love life. Jacob's transparency is refreshing and welcoming. His experience and passion are on full display. Anyone in need of some biblical, practical guidance will be blessed by this book.

Tim Valverde, Youth Pastor, Fountain of Truth Church, Fontana CA

SHIFT

Navigating through Faith, Life and Mission

A Guide for Young Adults

Jacob Rodriguez

Shift
© 2013 by Jacob M. Rodriguez

ISBN: 978-1-4903-5330-2

Emphasis within Scripture is the author's own. Please note that the author's writing style is to capitalize certain pronouns in Scripture and text that refer to God, and may differ from other religious publishers' styles. The author chose to acknowledge Him, even to the point of violating grammatical rules.

Dedication

This book is dedicated to my daughter, my princess Chloe Rodriguez, God's *early* gift to my family. I'm so proud to be your daddy.

Contents

Foreword

Someone once said, "The only constant in life is change." Everything will change. If you have lived long enough, you have come to the realization that things change. The interests you have will in one way or another change. Your values and priorities will change. Things that are important to you now, will more than likely not be as important as you go through the various stages of your life. Change is inevitable. You cannot avoid it, but you can make the appropriate adjustments to accommodate it.

As young adults our lives are constantly changing. We change career paths. We will even change majors a couple times before we complete a college degree. Relationships with our family, friends and people closest to us will change as the demands of life increase bringing with them added responsibilities and pressures. Change can be good or bad, depending on what we do with it.

Therefore, it is important that we learn how to navigate through these unexpected life alterations. This book that you are now reading is a life manual on how to handle the various transitions that you will go through in your young adult life. Pastor Jacob Rodriguez has carefully and creatively outlined the "shifts" that must take place if we are going to deepen our relationship with God, find solutions to life's difficult dilemmas, and become what God has created us to be.

We stand at a pivotal moment in our lives, critical to our advancement are the decisions that we make. This is important because our lives are the sum of our choices. We may not be able to control what life brings us, but we can make a conscious effort to respond correctly using the Word of God as our guide.

Our generation is plagued with a sense of entitlement. We believe that great things should happens to us simply because we want them to. What we fail to realize is that God has laid out life-altering principles in His Word that if we intentionally apply them to our specific situation, we will reap the rewards contained therein. The Bible was meant to be applied and not just simply read. It is for this reason that James 1:22 admonishes us to "… be doers of the Word…" (NKJV). If we are going to see all that God desires us to see, we must be willing to do something.

Shift is an invitation to experience God's best for your life. Allow the Spirit of God to take you on a journey toward fulfilling your God-given purpose. Let the insights contained on these pages lead you to a place of renewed vision and prophetic possibility. There are no limits to what you and I can accomplish if we will surrender the reins of our hearts and minds to the ultimate designer of our destinies, Jesus Christ Himself. Be encouraged, the best is yet to come!

Anthony Romo

Assistant Pastor, Phoenix First Apostolic Church

Phoenix, AZ

Introduction

The book you're holding was almost never written. Allow me to explain.

My journey as an author began eleven years ago after writing my first book, *The Woman's Touch*. I'll never forget my dad's look after I told him I was going to write a book to women. In fairness, it's not the typical conversation a dad (who is a pastor) has with his son. I don't blame him for wondering why I had not written a book to youth or young adults, since I was only 22-years-old at the time.

It seemed logical. In fact, I might have advised me to do the same. But I was in too deep. God had already placed a dire passion in me to minister to hurting women. So I went with it. God even allowed me to write a follow-up book entitled *The Lord's Lady*. I rejoice and redirect all praise and glory to God for the thousands of women who were reached.

But things have changed.

A couple of years ago, I wrote *Crave*, which was basically from my personal vault of devotions. It was a good change for me. I was able to express my thoughts in a context much different than my prior books. Another change was the audience. Instead of just women, it was directed to young adults.

After *Crave*, I began to tinker with idea of writing a full-length book to young singles and even the young marrieds. The only problem was I didn't know what the main topic would be. Needless to say, I crumpled up this project at least three times before I discovered the word - the concept that would define this book.

The word was *shift*.

Once this word marinated in my heart, the Holy Spirit began to unleash inspiration. *Shift* represents transition and change, something that every young adult is experiencing at some level.

Simply because that word stuck with me, I entitled this book "Shift" to capture the meaning of transition and to help you navigate through it. As you'll discover in the pages to come, Jesus Christ invites you to experience a life filled with purpose and passion. I believe this book will persuade you to shed patterns of the past and embrace your true potential. I hope it kindles a desire to know God, to let go of hurt and to fulfill your mission.

How to Read this Book

This book is written as a collection of essays and articles to help you navigate your way through faith, life and mission. It's best to approach each chapter as a separate conversation, so no need to wait for the last chapter to apply what you're learning about God and yourself.

You'll discover a good mix of storytelling, practicality, research and Biblical study. You'll also notice my conversational tone, which leads to some candid views and at times sheer transparency on my part. I believe you, as a young adult, need honest dialogue and raw truth, not just glossy lessons.

In this book, I've identified some crucial shifts and have grouped them under three broad categories:

1. Upward Shifts – these chapters will help you navigate your faith as you walk with Jesus and thrive in our culture.

2. Inward Shifts – these chapters will help you navigate your emotions and understand the basis of healthy relationships and dating.

3. Forward Shifts – these chapters will help navigate your mission and explore God's calling in your life.

In the bottom corners of my laptop keyboard is the "Shift" key, which only has one main function – to change things. Press the Shift key and you go from lower case to upper case letters and from numbers to symbols. At the end of each chapter you'll notice some "Shift Keys". These ideas are meant to be lighter fluids to fuel reflection, dialogue and prayer. In some cases, they are practical steps for you to follow.

Who Should Read this Book

Basically anyone can read this book. There is enough to feed every type of believer. However, this book is written specifically to young adults in their early-20's to mid-30's. That being said, not all the content of this book are ideal for teenagers as it is also written at a higher level of literacy.

I want to distinguish this fact because when people read the cover and see "a guide for young adults", they'll automatically assume "youth" and "teens". But quite honestly, this book is geared towards young adults in the college and career category.

If you're a teenager reading this, don't be discouraged. I dare you to read this book! No doubt, you will benefit from it.

If you're a married person, don't toss this book aside! You will find yourself pleasantly surprised at how God speaks to you. I'm married with a family myself; so it's written from that perspective.

If you're a parent, leader or pastor, this book can be a great tool for you to not only understand this generation but how to enhance your connection.

If you're in the target age group I mentioned, 20's and 30's, you MUST read this book cover to cover. You're the main reason I wrote it.

Apostolic Disclaimer

My theological stance throughout this book is boldly Oneness Apostolic. I don't hide my doctrine or affinity. I am who I am and care deeply about the Apostolic church, specifically *The Apostolic Assembly of the Faith in Christ Jesus*. Therefore, this book has been written with an Apostolic voice. Some of my views are slightly subjective but the truth is never compromised.

Now that the introduction and formalities are out of the way, I invite you to jump into this book and allow the Holy Spirit to work in your life.

Ready, set, *shift!*

Part One: Upward Shifts

1 | Friend Request
Fan to Follower

Have you accepted Jesus' *friend request?* In a culture of social media and enlarging circles of friends, you have to ask yourself if Jesus Christ is on the list. And if so, is He on the top of the list or lost in the clutter of tweets and status updates?

Like it or not, Facebook is not only woven into the tapestry of our culture but many would agree it has created a culture all its own. It's really quite fascinating how a website is able to connect millions of people all over the planet.

Whether you silently protest social media or update your Facebook status several times a day, I will assume that you are familiar with the term *Friend Request*. It's basically a request from someone to connect via Facebook or another social network.

There aren't any real ground rules for whom can *friend request* you—sometimes it comes from someone you know or met, and sometimes it's through a mutual friend. Other times it's from a complete stranger.

Amassing friends on Facebook has become somewhat of a sport for a lot of people, a race to see who can reach the highest number of *friends*. I remember when I reached 1,000 friends. I thought to myself, "Wow, do I really *know* all these people?" Of course, the answer was "no"; most are either acquaintances, people who want to follow my updates or those looking for free advertising. Whether online or in-person, true friendships still require time and effort to build.

The bottom-line is that Jesus wants to be your best friend. He's not interested in playing second-fiddle or being your rebound relationship. He wants to be your most intimate friend.

Your Secret Admirer

What makes Jesus different from any other friend is that He already knows you—inside and out. He knows your likes and dislikes, your desires and dreams, your struggles and fears. He knows where you've been, where you are, and even where you're going. He sees the intimate longings of your heart. Jesus knows the side of you that others don't. He knows your secrets: the secret crush you haven't told anyone about, the secret wound you've been nursing and of course the dark stuff, like pride, jealousy or lust. He knows what you like about yourself, and possibly what you hate.

He knows what makes you tick, what upsets you, what annoys you, what excites you, what makes you laugh, what makes you cry, what makes your heart race. He knows how you think and what you think, how you handle stress, how you cope with loss, how you react to difficult people and how you adapt to changing circumstances. He knows your needs and wants even before you ask.

King David was baffled at God's deep knowledge: "O Lord, You have searched me and known me. You know my sitting down and my rising up; You understand my thought afar off. You comprehend my path and my lying down, and are acquainted with all my ways. "For there is not a word on my tongue. But behold, O Lord, You know it altogether." (Psalm 139:1-4). Jesus knows your real status, not just the one you post on Facebook or Twitter. He knows your plans before you make them, your events before they happen.

As David wrote Psalm 139, I imagine he had to pause and let his mind drift in wonder. How could a cosmic God *know* and *care* about the microscopic details of human life?

God knows you better then you know yourself. The truth is, you can't even make sense of your own feelings sometimes. Like shoelaces, your emotions could be so knotted that you don't know how to untangle them. Or like a messy bedroom, your life could be so cluttered that there's not a clear pathway out. Sometimes we just ignore the mess because we're afraid of what we'll discover about ourselves or someone else. The reality is that humans are messy, especially compared to a holy and perfect God.

But here's some good news: *God has your back.* He's looking out for you.

Read what David said in Psalm 139:5: "You have hedged me behind and before, and laid Your hand upon me." Other Bible translations swap the word "hedged" for "hemmed", like a hem seals a garment from tearing and gives it a symmetrical finish. The word "hedged" in the original Hebrew language means, *enclose* or *encircle.* The word implies a fortified area as an aggressive military strategy to conquer a city. Maybe you're thinking, "Wait, are you saying God is trying to trap me?"

In a sense, yes, that's what I'm saying.

David's analogy describes God like a parent who confines his child to a playpen or fenced yard. God's desire is not to imprison you with barbed wire, but to lovingly encircle you with His grace.

Jesus is not like a "clingy" friend who always drops by uninvited or can't take a hint. Clingy friends smother you. Jesus is also not a stalker or someone who invades your privacy or snoops around like a burglar. Jesus is a perfect gentleman. In fact, Revelations 3:20 portrays Jesus as one who is knocking at your door waiting for you to hear His voice and invite Him in.

Think of Jesus more as your secret admirer. According to Wikipedia, a secret admirer "is an individual who feels adoration, fondness or love for another person without disclosing their identity to that person. The admirer may often send gifts or love letters to their crush. A secret admirer is usually benign. Mostly, the goal of a secret admirer is to woo the object of their affections, and then to reveal their identity, paving the way for a real relationship." [1]

Think about this. God loves you and yet He doesn't reveal too much, too soon. He sends you gifts of grace, hoping it will lure your heart closer. His love letter is the Bible—containing over 3,000 promises and hundreds of love notes. As you draw closer to Jesus, He will reveal more of Himself. He invites you to delight in Him, to savor Him, to love Him with all your being.

James 4:8 says, "Draw near to God and He will draw near to you..." If you pursue God, He'll let you find Him. He's not going to play cat-and-mouse with you. If you seek Him, you'll find Him. As you gravitate towards God, He will return the favor. However, it's the second half of James 4:8 that may put a damper on things: "...Cleanse your hands, you sinners; and

---

[1] "Secret admirer." *Wikipedia: The Free Encyclopedia.* Wikimedia Foundation, Inc. 13 February 2013. Web. 4 April 2013

purify your hearts, you double-minded."

Say what? Cleanse? Purify?

Can't we just know God, download some answered prayers and blessings and just leave the other half of our lives alone? Not really. I believe you're going to discover a God who calls us to throw caution against the wind, love him radically and allow Him total access into our lives.

God of Everything

In an age of disposable relationships and "friends with benefits", loyalty has become an endangered virtue. It seems this generation hardly knows what it means to be loyal. Instead, our culture embraces a *no strings attached* philosophy where relationships don't have any boundaries or restrictions. This cultural disposition has spilled over into Christianity. Young believers tend to approach their relationship with Christ in similar fashion. They want a relationship that's not too demanding, too restrictive or too costly. And sadly, this has robbed many people of a genuine relationship with God.

Let's read James 4:8 again, this time in the New Living Translation: "Come close to God, and God will come close to you. Wash your hands, you sinners; purify your hearts, for your loyalty is divided between God and the world." We can easily fix our eyes on the words "wash" and "purify". But the root issue is *divided loyalty*, which leads to sinful choices and conduct.

There must be a shift in our relationship with God, or a "RelationShift". This requires a revolution of thought and practice, a fresh encounter with truth.

As true followers of Jesus Christ, we must be willing to forsake ourselves and commit every area of our lives to Him.

We can't compartmentalize God. Basically, that means we can't just *fit* God into our lives like the way you sort your clothes in the closet or organize your apps on your iPhone. Too often we create compartments in our lives such as *social*, *financial*, and *spiritual*. Then we pat ourselves on the back because we gave God His own special compartment in our hearts.

It was never God's idea that we create these categories. The ancient Hebrews did not view spirituality as a separate compartment from the rest of life, but *all* of life was to be lived with *all* of God. Actually, devout Jews recited that principle twice a day in what's called the *Shema* (see Deut. 6:4-9), emphasizing how God permeated everything in life.

God doesn't just want strings attached.

He prefers to be the main thread that's woven into the fabric of our lives.

Follow = Fall Low

In order to *follow* Jesus, you must *fall low*—in humility, self-denial, and reckless abandonment. In the words of John the Baptist, "He must increase, but I *must* decrease" (John 3:30). His increase is proportionate to my decrease. The more I decrease, the more Jesus increases.

Jesus' invitation to become His friend is really an invitation become His follower. In the eyes of Jesus, a friend and a follower are synonymous. In other words, you can't claim to be His friend and then choose not to follow Him. Too many of us want fellowship without followership. A self-professed Christian (friend of Jesus) who doesn't follow Him totally is not actually a friend at all.

When Jesus sends us a friend request, He's actually inviting us to follow Him. As I stated in my book *Crave*, "Our *followership* determines our *fellowship* with Jesus. In other words, how we follow Christ affects our relationship with Him." I believe the story of the rich young ruler illustrates the tension that young adults often feel between being a friend (follower) of Jesus, and just being a fan of Jesus.

Jesus sent this young man the ultimate friend request. We find this story in Mark 10:17-22:

> "Now as He was going out on the road, one came
> running, knelt before Him, and asked Him, 'Good

Teacher, what shall I do that I may inherit eternal life?' So Jesus said to him, 'Why do you call Me good? No one *is* good but One, *that is,* God. You know the commandments: *Do not commit adultery, Do not murder, Do not steal, Do not bear false witness,* Do not defraud, *Honor your father and your mother.*' And he answered and said to Him, 'Teacher, all these things I have kept from my youth.' Then Jesus, looking at him, loved him, and said to him, 'One thing you lack: Go your way, sell whatever you have and give to the poor, and you will have treasure in heaven; and come, take up the cross, and follow Me.' But he was sad at this word, and went away sorrowful, for he had great possessions."

Like many believers today, this young man walked a religious path, but couldn't let go of his own self-interests and ambitions. To his credit, he seemed very sincere. When meeting Jesus, he knelt and called him the "good teacher". But his bubble was burst when Jesus asked him to donate all his possessions to the poor and follow Him. This young man wanted a revelation, but Jesus wanted a relationship. And what he didn't realize is that revelation is a byproduct of relationship.

The young rich ruler was a fan of Jesus. If Jesus had a fan page on Facebook, this young guy would have clicked on the "Like" button. If Jesus had Twitter, this guy would have ironically clicked the "follow" button, but to become a friend of Jesus is to follow him as a disciple.

Jesus said in Luke 14:27: "And whoever does not bear his cross and come after Me cannot be My disciple." A few verses later He said, "So likewise, whoever of you does not forsake all that he has cannot be My disciple." To accept Jesus' friend request is to forsake everything and carry a cross.

The rich young ruler couldn't see his life inside of God's circle. Why?

Because instead of celebrating everything he would gain, he only focused on what he had to lose. Satan wants to convince you that following Jesus is reclusive and drudgery. However, Jesus said: "Come to Me, all *you* who labor and are heavy laden, and I will give you rest. Take My yoke upon you and learn from Me, for I am gentle and lowly in heart, and you will find rest for your souls. For My yoke *is* easy and My burden is light" (Matt. 11:28-30).

Life outside the circle seems liberating for a moment, but you quickly realize that you're defenseless against the railing attacks of Satan. Living in God's circle doesn't mean you won't make mistakes or commit any sins. It doesn't mean you become perfect or invincible. It does mean, however, that when you step into a mess or a trap that you won't be alone.

God's circle of friends and followers are found in the secret place.

In Psalm 91:1 we read, "He who dwells in the secret place of the Most High shall abide under the shadow of the Almighty." In verse 14, the Lord declares, "Because he has set his love upon Me, therefore I will deliver him; I will set him on high, because he has known My name." In other words, because of a genuine relationship, He will bail you out of trouble and elevate your life above the ordinary. By accepting God's friend request, which is a call to forsake and follow (fall low), you are positioned for God's kingdom purpose.

Fan Clubs

When Jesus said, *"follow me"*, He wasn't merely talking about where He walked, but how He lived. In other words, He says, "Do *what* I do. Shadow Me. Pray *like* Me. Act *like* Me. Suffer *like* Me." Following Jesus is a call to imitate His life. It's more than just wearing a *WWJD* wristband. It's bearing the cross and becoming like Him. In his book, *Not a Fan*, author Kyle Idleman describes how fans think:

> "One way fans try to follow Jesus without denying themselves is by compartmentalizing the areas of their lives they don't want him to have access to. They try to negotiate the terms of the deal. 'I'll follow Jesus, but

I'm not going to sell my possessions. Don't ask me to forgive the people who hurt me; they don't deserve that. Don't ask me to save sex for marriage; I can't help my desires. Don't ask me to give a percentage of my money; I worked hard for that cash.' And instead of following Jesus with their financial life, they follow Money magazine. In their relationships, instead of Jesus they follow Oprah."[2]

Accepting Jesus' friend request and following Him requires a total commitment. The young ruler wanted to have it both ways. His heart was torn in two. His loyalty was divided. His priorities were out of order.

The gospel of Luke describes three encounters that Jesus had with three *would-be* followers: "Now it happened as they journeyed on the road, that someone said to Him, 'Lord, I will follow You wherever You go.' And Jesus said to him, 'Foxes have holes and birds of the air have nests, but the Son of Man has nowhere to lay His head.' Then He said to another, 'Follow Me.' But he said, 'Lord, let me first go and bury my father.' Jesus said to him, 'Let the dead bury their own dead, but you go and preach the kingdom of God.' And another also said, 'Lord, I will follow You, but let me first go and bid them farewell who

---

[2] Idleman, Kyle (2011-05-24). Not a Fan: Becoming a Completely Committed Follower of Jesus (p. 146). Zondervan. Kindle Edition.

are at my house.' But Jesus said to him, 'No one, having put his hand to the plow, and looking back, is fit for the kingdom of God'" (Luke 9:57-62).

These three aspiring disciples encountered Jesus at the pinnacle of His popularity. If political polls existed, His favorability rate would have soared. But Jesus didn't want a fan club or cheerleaders. He wanted real followers, real friends. These three guys offer one of the most pixilated pictures of *fans* in the New Testament.

Fan #1 – Wanted to follow

This guy had grand expectations. He saw an opportunity to jump on the bandwagon. Matthew's version of the story says he was a scribe (See Matt. 8:19). Perhaps he saw an intellectual advantage. He and Jesus could brew some coffee and talk about theology and politics. Maybe he saw a financial advantage. He could go on tour with Jesus and get VIP treatment.

Whatever his assumptions were, they came crashing down when Jesus said He had *nowhere to lay His head*. Jesus wasn't speaking literally (he had places to sleep), but figuratively. He wanted to emphasize the cost of following Him. In other words, you cannot be attached to the things of this world.

God is asking this generation, "Are you willing to live without certain comforts? Can you handle rejection and possibly having your heart broken?"

Fan #2 – Invited to follow

Unlike fan #1, Jesus personally invited this guy. This is significant because it means that Jesus hand-selected him, despite whatever flaws or issues he might have had. Jesus called him out. But his excuse was a little pathetic. On the surface, it seems reasonable for him to decline Jesus' offer. His story was that his father died and he had to bury him first. If there was a legitimate excuse, this would be it. What kind of loving God wouldn't let a grieving son bury his father? But hold on. There were some obvious holes in his story.

The burial customs of Palestine were to bury the dead on the same day they died. If his father had actually died that day, why would he be wasting time by lollygagging and following crowds? I'm speculating of course. But the real issue with fan #2 was *priority*.

I think Jesus got bothered by the word *first*—"Lord, let me *first* go and bury my father" (emphasis mine). In other words, "Lord, let me focus on what's important—school, career, family, friends, boyfriend/girlfriend, money—then I'll dedicate what's leftover." This attitude is insulting to God. It demotes Him to playing second-string or riding in the back seat of your life. School, career, friends and so on are all important. Get an education, become a professional, make a lot of friends—as long as Jesus is first and foremost in your life. He instructed us in Matthew 6:33 to "seek first the kingdom of God".

Jesus is calling you to reorder your life. He doesn't just want to be a picture frame, the structure that's holding everything together. Jesus wants to be the artist that colors your world with His purpose and promises. He also wants to be the focal point of the portrait. If you're going to be a friend of God, a follower of Jesus Christ, He must become your highest priority.

Fan #3 – Wanted to follow, but...

The final fan just went with the flow and borrowed the excuses from fans 1 and 2. Since both chickened out, it made his decision a little easier. If both had said yes to Jesus, he might have gone for it. Fan #3, it seems, felt more comfortable with the crowds. He followed the trend.

We tend to be easily motivated by popularity. If something is widely believed or followed, a young adult feels the pressure to conform and be socially accepted by his peers.

Based on the first two excuses, the validity of the last excuse is questionable. But for the sake of argument, let's assume the following statement is true: "Lord, I will follow You, but let me first go and bid them farewell who are at my house." Again the word "first" appears.

But if fan #3 was being honest, then it seems he was afraid to leave the familiar. He felt some separation anxiety. He wasn't comfortable leaving his nest—mom and dad, brothers and sisters, close friends and family. Maybe he was coddled by mom (i.e. momma's boy) or worked in the family business.

Some young adults prolong "growing up" because they have it made at home – lots of freedom but little responsibility (no rent and free food). They enjoy occasional encounters with God but have the habit of running back whenever pressure boils. They piggyback on their parent's prayers and hide behind them when challenges come knocking.

I learned that when you're placed in hot water like a tea bag, you discover what's in you. If you avoid real challenges, you'll never release your hidden potential.

Imagine if all three of these candidates would have accepted Jesus' friend request and followed Him? It could have been "Jesus and the 15 Disciples". I guess we'll never know.

Confirm or Not Now

When you receive a friend request on Facebook, you have the choice of clicking "*Confirm*" or "*Not Now*". If you click "not now", you're basically ignoring the request—either because you don't really know the person or you're just not interested.

As you turn the pages of this book, you'll realize that accepting God's friend request is more than just clicking a button and posting prayers on His wall. Jesus invites you into a close friendship, a loving relationship that centers on the glorious Gospel—His death, burial and resurrection.

With His death and resurrection, Jesus made it possible for us to be forgiven of our sins and has invited us to be His friends. In case you're not aware, you have a friend request from Jesus sitting in your inbox.

Click "*Accept*" today.

Shift Keys

1. **Accept God's friendship** – Jesus made the ultimate friend request by coming to earth and saying "come unto me". He committed the ultimate act of love by dying on the cross for your sins. If you haven't accepted Jesus as your friend, accept Him today and start a personal relationship.

2. **Change your priorities** – The three *would-be* disciples in this chapter all shied away from following Jesus because other things were more important. If your friendship with Jesus has been neglected or cluttered, it's time to shuffle your priorities and make sure Jesus is first in your life. In Matthew 6:33, Jesus said, "But seek first the kingdom of God and His righteousness, and all these things shall be added to you."

3. **Leave the familiar** – God is calling you to step outside your comfort zone to discover the adventure of *followership*. Maybe you've been playing it safe for too long and sense that now is the time to experience a new level of faith. Maybe you're stuck in spiritual survival mode and yearn for something beyond casual Christianity. If so, it's time to do something about it. By God's grace, you can shift into your destiny.

2 | Generation Me

Selfish to Selfless

We live in a society that promises instant gratification, immediate results and a "no assembly required" approach and convinces you that you're the center of the universe. Everything from modern parenting, education to personal technology, this generation has been pampered unlike any other in history. Because everyone seems so afraid to face bad feelings, it creates a culture of artificial success, where "honor student" awards are handed out alphabetically (instead of based on merit) and everyone gets a trophy (winners *and* losers).

The reality is, if everyone gets a trophy, no one wins and no one experiences the agony of defeat.

Our generation also has a warped understanding of disappointment and hard work. Our idea of disappointment is when the barista at Starbucks messes up our order, when we realize we're not as popular or well liked as we thought, when we're asked to do more than expected and basically when we don't get what we want.

In the world of Facebook, where everybody is your "friend", we nearly collapse when we learn that we have an enemy or two. Maybe it's because you've been so sheltered from reality that normal life, with all its hurts and failures amounts to what seems like the end of the world.

Many young adults born in the 1980s or early 1990s (myself included) are referred to as Generation Y or Millennials and are considered to be the most entitled, self-focused and narcissistic generation in American history. In his book *Generation iY: Our Last Chance to Save Their Future*, Dr. Tim Elmore identified some aspects that would make it difficult for Millennials to enter adult reality. I've listed some of them below, but with my own definitions:

1. **Artificial** – Many young adults spend much of their time online, living vicariously through Facebook, Twitter or Instagram. I would simply label this an "unlife", an unreal life that inhibits real relationships and social development. The virtual world allows you to create versions of yourself that can be easily manipulated.

2. **Homogeneous** – Dr. Elmore's research indicates that Millennials spend the majority of their time with other Millennials—over 50 percent of their day with peers and only 15 percent with older adults.[3] Isn't this true? Don't we tend to flock together by age group? It seems we need a broader scope of social interaction that allows older generations to connect with us, guide us and prepare us. You should definitely rethink your day-to-day activities and figure out how you can include older adults in your life, besides your parents.

3. **Guaranteed** – Some of us have been raised in a fail-proof environment. But too much protection can stunt your maturity and foster an attitude of entitlement. You can't go through life expecting mom or dad to write a check for all your bad decisions. You will never grow that way. Not everything in life is risk-free and guaranteed.

4. **Programmed** – You might be the product of an over-programmed, over-structured childhood. That's good in some ways because it puts you on a stable course. But as you get older, it could prevent your ability to

---

[3] Elmore, Dr. Tim (2010-11-01). Generation iY: Our Last Chance to Save Their Future (Kindle Locations 812-824). Poet Gardener. Kindle Edition.

interpret life and make strong decisions. Sometimes you can't wait for a general consensus or a paved road before you move.

5. **Narcissistic** – Maybe all the self-esteem rhetoric of the 80's and 90's backfired because overall, this generation is very egocentric and self-aware. I know it's easy to label someone a narcissist without knowing them personally. But it's hard to argue that our culture is not self-obsessed in many ways. Please understand, however, that *hating* yourself is not the answer. Jesus taught that love of self must be counterweighted with love for others (See Mark 12:31).

Dr. Elmore's diagnosis of Generation Y is an eye-opener for everyone, young and old. Since the author is writing from a secular viewpoint, I would add another aspect to this list:

6. **Religious** – My observation is that many young adults have been programmed to believe that it's primarily the church's job to feed them spiritually and meet all their needs. Bibles are carried, not read. Plus, they are nurtured to think that showing up for church activities is the definition of Christian maturity.

The trend of the current generation is not benign, but has silently spread into the mentality of many young adult believers who see their world and mission with the same cultural lenses that non-believers do. Therefore a radical shift is needed, one that revives our passion for God and compassion for the unsaved and underserved.

I suggest we stop looking for Christian superheroes or celebrity preachers to give us the answer. All we need to do is follow Jesus and His example.

Grow Up Like Jesus

If anyone in history had a right to act entitled, it was Jesus. He is the Son of God, the Messiah, the image of the invisible God, the God-man, the King of kings, the Lord of lords, the Savior, the Word made flesh. Jesus was more than entitled; he was enthroned. Yet his life resembles that of a working-class, blue-collar tradesman whose childhood was typical of any Jewish family.

A closer look at Jesus' human development should give you some fresh perspective.

Jesus was subject to his parents

As a young man, Jesus honored his parents and never attempted to usurp their authority. When Joseph and Mary found Jesus, who was 12-years-old, studying and teaching at the temple, He obeyed their rules and returned home (See Luke 2:41-42). Since Jesus already understood and sensed His "father's business", it seems reasonable for Him to completely step out in His purpose.

Why hang out at home and work at a dusty carpentry shop when you're called, gifted and able to chase your dreams? Well, Jesus not only respected traditional Jewish values, but He was wise enough to know that it wasn't His time. Read what Luke 2:50 says: "But they did not understand the statement which He spoke to them." Jesus and His parents didn't see eye-to-eye. It was like they were speaking two different languages.

Sounds familiar? I'm sure you can relate.

Jesus had a choice in this situation. He could have overstepped human boundaries and overextended his divine authority. But the Bible says Jesus "…went down with them and came to Nazareth, and was subject to them, but His mother kept all these things in her heart" (Luke 2:51). Jesus was entitled to do whatever he wanted. Instead he honored his parents and went back to real life.

Jesus increased in wisdom and stature

After the incident at the temple and Jesus went home, the Bible says, "Jesus increased in wisdom and stature" (Luke 2:52). In our culture, there's a notion that wisdom and personal growth happens when you leave home and experiment with life. You're egged on by the world to splurge, indulge and explore everything possible. After a few sexual encounters, a college frat party, an unplanned trip to Las Vegas, a political rally and a few vampire novels, you're supposed to be wiser and smarter.

Not so much.

The truth is, if you're overexposed you might actually become dumber. I was going to be nicer and say, "become...*less wise*", but that just doesn't do it justice. The reality is, this generation seems to be getting dumber – maybe not about technology, but certainly about life. That's not an insult, just an honest viewpoint.

Jesus increased in wisdom and stature after he went home. This is where I draw a connection between living under authority (with some restraint) and increased wisdom. Of course, if your college or career has moved you away from home, that's a reasonable scenario. However, by *home*, I'm not merely referring to your parent's house so much as their influence in your life. Home can also represent a church, mentor or pastor who can give you real direction and covering.

Basically, you should stop looking for wisdom among your peers, but in places and people who have a wealth of experience and discernment.

Jesus increased in favor with God and men

Jesus found favor by being under the umbrella of His parents and choosing a simple life. In His humanity, being fully man, Jesus lived a life that attracted vertical and horizontal favor. The author Luke is not downplaying the deity of Jesus, but simply pointing out that Jesus grew up without special privileges and that He found heavenly favor.

In addition, Jesus found earthly favor. He was obedient to laws and customs. He was honest and respectful. Jesus demonstrated an ability to grow spiritually and also humanly. He experienced life at your stage.

Contrast that against this generation that feels entitled to every available pleasure and privilege that society has to offer. In general terms, Millennials want something for nothing. They want handouts. They want to spend money without making it. They want sex without marriage. They want instant fame.

Even churchgoers have a set of entitlements. They want ministry without discipline. They want miracles and wonders without prayer and fasting. They want titles without responsibilities. They want to be served. They want to be entertained.

Again, I'm speaking in general terms. So, of course there are exceptions. I'm delighted to see many young men and women who are focusing themselves and seeking the Kingdom of God. But part of this book is simply a response to what is still a growing problem in all corners of society –young adults who are not growing up or contributing, much less changing the world.

The Gift of Hard Work

Jesus' human development involved traditional roles and responsibilities. He established himself as a stable young man long before He preached His first recorded sermon or turned water into wine. An often-overlooked side of Jesus' life is who He was and what He did prior to His public ministry. For Him to launch out with such effectiveness was not only because He was the Son of God, but He developed himself as the Son of Man.

What does that mean, exactly?

Jesus had a job.

Biblical scholars speculate on whether Jesus was actually a carpenter, citing that there's no definitive proof. But there are enough hints to strongly suggest He was. His trade as a carpenter created skepticism early in his ministry: "Is this not the carpenter, the Son of Mary, and brother of James, Joses, Judas, and Simon? And are not His sisters here with us?" So they were offended at Him" (Mark 6:3).

Since formal business schools didn't exist, Jesus didn't get a degree in business administration, organizational leadership or even finance. But in order to run a small business, he would have had general business skills such as accounting to consider the costs of goods and labor, supply and demand, pricing, the cost of maintenance and replacement of equipment. This wasn't the Home Depot, but certainly even a small mom-and-pop shop required some business sense.

Before Jesus became a professional, He would have interned under Joseph, His step-dad. He learned the tools and tricks of the trade. He sweated. He ran errands. He delivered a product. He worked.

Ecclesiastes 9:10 may not ever be chosen as a youth camp or conference theme, but I happen to think it's the glue that could make your dreams stick. Here's what it says: "Whatever your hand finds to do, do it with all your might, for in the realm of the dead, where you are going, there is neither working nor planning, nor knowledge, nor wisdom" (NIV).

The writer, presumably King Solomon, wrapped up human existence in what feels like the sad ending of a movie. Basically, "Work hard because once you're dead, that's it. No more work, scheduling, client meetings, bills, or anything else to learn." His forlorn tone is not to sadden you, but actually to inspire you like an elderly man who's about to die and has some final words of wisdom.

What Solomon is not saying is, "do whatever you want". If so, it becomes a license to sin or rebel against God's Word. On the contrary, he is urging young adults to apply themselves and work hard towards a goal. If you are a student, study hard. If you are employed, work hard and don't cheat your company. If you are involved in a ministry at your church, serve well.

Many Millennials suffer from what I'll call the *someday syndrome*, a tendency to procrastinate or attempt to fix all the world's problems instead doing one or two things well. We love to theorize and discuss. We start projects and don't finish them. We tinker with ideas that never materialize. Solomon is sending this generation a wake-up call and saying, "Get to work, because once we've died and gone to heaven, it's too late."

Consider the following Scriptures:

- And whatever you do, do it heartily, as to the Lord and not to men, knowing that from the Lord you will receive the reward of the inheritance; for you serve the Lord Christ. (Colossians 3:23-24)

- And there are diversities of activities, but it is the same God who works all in all. (1 Cor. 12:6)

- But let each one examine his own work, and then he will have rejoicing in himself alone, and not in another. For each one shall bear his own load. (Galatians 6:4-5)

- In all labor there is profit, but idle chatter *leads* only to poverty. (Proverbs 14:23)

- The fool folds his hands and consumes his own flesh. (Eccl. 4:5)

- If anyone will not work, neither shall he eat. (2 Thess. 3:10)

This section opened with the header, "The Gift of Hard Work". Most of us don't consider hard work a gift. But when you work, you discover powerful secrets about God and yourself. You invite God's favor into your life, because God Himself is a worker. He's not a theorist; He's a doer, an inventor.

From Experiencers to Doers

Although it's important to recognize your identity *in* Christ, you should not neglect your works *for* Christ. The apostle Paul said, "For we are His workmanship, created in Christ Jesus for good works, which God prepared beforehand that we should walk in them" (Ephesians 2:10).

Somewhere along the way, we've downgraded "works" and replaced it solely with "identity". Yet we must understand that works flow from identity. In other words, your *who* determines your *do*. If all you do is celebrate who you are and never work at something, you are not living life as God intended. The God of the cosmos, the great I AM didn't sit back and say, "I'm special and that's all that matters." Not even close. God is a God of work, of action, of doing. When He created the heavens and earth, He worked His plan for six days straight and then rested on the seventh day. We tend to reverse that philosophy – work one day and take six days off.

Don't wait for work to come to you. Go after it. Whether it's related to academics, vocation, or ministry, go after it!

Part of the problem is that we have become a generation of "experiencers" and have lost the gift of innovation and hard work. You might be like many young adults who are experiencers of life. Experiencers depend on circumstances, staged opportunities and basically wait for things to go their way. They want to walk into places that have already been built and created. They want to be served. They want to amuse themselves like visitors in an art gallery. Let's be honest, we all love great experiences. There's nothing inherently wrong with them. But if all you do is go from experience to experience, you will never realize your ability to dream, to create and to build.

People always ask me, "Jacob, how can I write a book?"

I smile and say, "Start writing".

We always want a magical answer to doing things. After I respond, I usually get that confused look, as if I just told a kid that Santa Claus wasn't real. I get the sense they wanted to hear something profound, something deep and mystical. The real spiritual ones want me to say I've spent hundreds of hours praying about the book before writing it. However, I don't pray for books – I pray to pray, to draw closer to the Lord. I don't have a special "book prayer". The Holy Spirit just leads me as I begin to write.

The real intellectual ones want me to say that I've spent countless hours studying, researching and philosophizing in a cozy library next to a crackling fireplace. Of course, I read and research (which you find in this book), but it's balanced. Maybe if I wrote Medical textbooks that would be different. The ambitious ones want me to recommend two or three books on "how to write a book", which software to use besides Microsoft Word (because that seems too amateur), and the names and numbers of all my publishing contacts.

My thoughts are – why do you need all of that to *start* writing? See my point?

Eventually, you have to stop picturing and start practicing. Stop just experiencing things and start making things with the gifts that God has given you. And you guessed it. That means rolling up your sleeves and getting to work.

Shaking the Shiftless

I came across a scripture that caught my attention. Being that the title of this book is *Shift*, I really believe the Holy Spirit led me to Proverbs 19:15 (NIV): "Laziness brings on deep sleep, and the shiftless go hungry." Honestly, this wasn't a scripture I had jotted down or studied before writing this book. It's so small and similar to dozens of other proverbs. Yet, it echoed in my heart.

The term *laziness* doesn't sound very intellectual. But it's very Biblical. And to me it seems young adults are getting lazier.

Laziness incubates within the entitlement culture – "generation me". It creates the perfect climate for a *what's in it for me?* mentality.

Let's zoom in on Proverbs 19:15 for a moment. Please, read it again.

Many lazy and entitled young adults waste their years hiding behind rationalizations and fear. Therefore laziness induces a spiritual coma and making you incapable of taking responsibility. Lazy and entitled people may listen to voices in their mind that say:

- "You're doing just fine; why accept a new challenge?
- "Your mom and dad pray; just take your time to start a prayer life."
- "As long as you like yourself, you don't have to improve yourself."
- "You're not as bad as some *other* people."

- "I don't need college. Bill Gates, Steve Jobs and Mark Zuckerberg *didn't* graduate college."

What's most startling about Proverbs 19:15 is the second half: "the shiftless go hungry". In other words, those young adults who refuse to shift or make necessary changes find themselves empty and desperate. Those unwilling to shift priorities, relationships and goals will discover a life of broken dreams and insignificance.

Instead of shifting into work mode, young adults today are consumed with purposeless activity such as Facebook and other social medias. Young ladies starving for attention and purpose will use their sexuality instead of choosing chastity. Young men starving for adventure will spend hours playing video games instead of making a real difference.

There is a price to pay for doing nothing, for being complacent. As a young adult, maybe it's time for a self-evaluation. Are you busy, but not productive? Do you quit easily?

These questions might shake you a little. But that's ok.

You see, God wants His church to be empowered, not entitled. Jesus said the following: "But you shall receive power when the Holy Spirit has come upon you; and you shall be witnesses to Me in Jerusalem, and in all Judea and Samaria, and to the end of the earth" (Acts 1:8). If we're going to shake the world with gospel of Jesus Christ, we need to be shifted from entitlement to empowerment, from selfish to selfless, from waiting to working.

Shift Keys

1. Get under authority – Jesus honored his parents and never attempted to undermine their authority. By submitting yourself to authority, you attract God's favor and wisdom, and establish a culture of discipline. The entitlement mentality has to be fixed from the ground up, which is an undefined relationship between generations.

2. Be known for what you do – Knowing your identity is so important, but don't stop there. Good reputations are built by what you do. Paul urged young Timothy to "Let no one despise your youth, but be an **example** to the believers in word, in **conduct**, in love, in spirit, in faith, in purity" (1 Tim. 4:12, my emphasis). Be a doer, a builder, a creator and a person of action.

3. Raise the bar – Many lazy and entitled young adults waste precious years by hiding behind rationalizations and fears. Pursue excellence and go beyond what's expected or required of you. Don't allow low expectations to define your potential. It's human nature to choose the path of least resistance, to settle for less. Do something that forces you to face your fears and depend more on God.

3 | Decoding Culture

Regular to Peculiar

In an age of moral relativism and cultural decadence, there is a need for young adults to boldly live for Christ. But what does that mean, exactly? Does it mean you are supposed to wear Christian t-shirts, vote Republican and bump Christian rock music in your car? Does it mean that you should become vegan, give peace a chance and be an advocate for human rights? Or does it mean to become Amish, reject technology and innovation and live as a recluse? It seems living boldly for Christ in our culture is defined differently based on who you ask.

I humbly suggest that Christianity doesn't need to be overly-contextualized or attached to one particular cause or movement. For you to thrive as a Christ-follower in our culture, let's observe what Jesus said in John 15:19 (NIV): "If you belonged to the world, it would love you as its own. As it is, you do not belong to the world, but I have chosen you out of the world. That is why the world hates you." The key to living in the world is remembering that you are *not of this world*. I know the phrase "Not of this World" has become a popular cliché. But let's embrace the real meaning of it.

In this chapter, I want to offer some insight into our culture and how you, as a young adult, can thrive without losing your identity.

Campus Culture

One of the great cultural battlegrounds is found in Academia, on college and university campuses across America. As more Apostolic young adults attend and graduate from college, this presents new opportunities for success that prior generations could not achieve. This is a promising sign of future growth and prosperity within the Church.

For Hispanics in particular, higher education is a relatively new territory compared to other ethnic groups. You might very well be the first generation in your family to attend college or earn a degree. If so, that's exciting. You should pursue higher learning and achieve success with the blessing of God's favor.

However, there is another side to this shift that needs to be discussed. If you are in college or have attended college, you have already been exposed to a plethora of human philosophies and intellectualism. You have already encountered humanism and anti-biblical science.

At East Palo Alto Apostolic Church where I currently serve as English Pastor, many of our young adults are college students or have already graduated. I thank God for one young lady in particular who often approaches me with tough questions. Sometimes the questions are for her to answer classmates and professors who challenge her Biblical worldview.

Honestly, it's much easier to respond with some weak cookie-cutter answers. But if your only response is, "because the Bible says", your classmates and professors will easily pick your argument apart. Of course, if the Bible says something, that stands on its own. But you should seek to know *where* it says it and *why* it says it. Interestingly, you can also synchronize science, math and literature with Scripture to further prove your points.

We have to engage skeptics and agnostics head-on instead of viewing them as a lost cause. Don't feel pressured to know *everything* in the Bible or be an expert. You obviously have to spend your time studying your college coursework to ensure you get good grades. But in order to thrive spiritually, you must have a solid foundation and at least know what to expect.

Pop Culture

Besides campus culture, there is also pop culture, which continues to replenish itself with reality TV shows like *Jersey Shore* and *Keeping Up with the Kardashians*. Although pop culture extends far beyond networks like MTV, this entertainment and cultural powerhouse certainly pioneered the sexualization of young people in our country. Back in the 80's and 90's, MTV introduced Americans to some of the most lewd and vulgar entertainment ever seen on TV.

However, fast forward twenty years and those early MTV shows look more like *Little House on the Prairie* compared to what's broadcast today—on TV and the Internet.

Film and literature continue to experiment on the minds of young adults who crave the next big thing. For instance, *The Twilight* saga (books and movies) is a vampire and romance phenomenon that has captured the hearts and minds of millions. Tethered to his genre is a growing fascination with the occult, the paranormal and horror. Millions of people are voluntarily traumatizing themselves with images of erotic torture. It's no wonder why violence and aggression is on the rise. Our culture is becoming more and more desensitized to violence and graphic images.

This is a spiritual battle.

The enemy is at work in our society in ways that most

people don't realize or care to know. As we pray, fast and maintain our devotion, our eyes must be open to the hidden dangers that lurk in our world. If ever there was a time to live boldly for Christ and the Bible, it's now. As a surge of strategies are hatched to dismantle Christian values in nearly every arena of our culture, we must confront these challenges with God's truth and grace.

As a young adult, you can't walk through this world like a dry sponge, freely absorbing everything our culture throws at you. In college, you're likely to experience a collision course of ideas, lifestyles and philosophies that will challenge your views and convictions. Don't be afraid. If you are filled with the Holy Spirit, then you have been empowered to overcome the obstacles and temptations of this world. The apostle Paul urges us in the following way:

"Do not conform to the pattern of this world, but be transformed by the renewing of your mind. Then you will be able to test and approve what God's will is—His good, pleasing and perfect will" (Romans 12:2 NIV).

The message is clear. Don't imitate the world's pattern of living. A pattern is a design or a mold that replicates itself for purpose of conformity. That would describe how our world operates. It's a system that clones its ideologies and beliefs through education and entertainment.

We are instructed not to imitate the world's pattern, but to live in contrast by showing what true love and peace is all about. The mold is broken when we embody the mission of Jesus Christ and allow our lights to shine. As the apostle Peter said: "But you are a chosen generation, a royal priesthood, a holy nation, His own special people, that you may proclaim the praises of Him who called you out of darkness into His marvelous light" (1 Peter 2:9).

The word "special" in this verse means peculiar, odd or weird. Maybe that sounds strange to you, but it simply emphasizes that we are God's special possession – an uncommon people who are citizens of a Heavenly culture.

In other words, my physical location is on earth, but my spiritual identity and citizenship is in the Kingdom of God. You are God's child, not a clone of society. You are not some regular person, but a peculiar person with an incredible destiny.

That's why being a follower of Jesus changes your life. You have been marked by God and no matter how hard you try to blend into the world, you will never fit in. You will never be a happy sinner, because deep within, you will hear the calling of God and know that you have been created with divine purpose.

Strainer vs. Sponge

Maybe it's time your trade your sponge for a strainer. My coffee maker illustrates this idea. It has an internal system that irrigates the filter containing raw coffee grounds. As hot water pumps and fills the filter, the pure coffee then pours from the filter into the carafe. I'm such a coffee lover that I can practically smell the aroma as I type.

Anyhow, the filter (strainer) is the most important component because it keeps the grainy coffee grounds out and permits the drinkable coffee to pour out.

Here's the point: when encountering culture, become a filter, a strainer – meaning you redeem the good and reject the bad. For instance, not all technology is evil – therefore redeem the good and reject the bad. Not all forms of entertainment are evil – therefore redeem the good and reject the bad. And if the Holy Spirit is living within you, you'll be able to discern and make better choices.

All You Can Eat

When you encounter God, become a sponge. Absorb everything about Him – His ways, His truth and His life. The Bible is an all-you-can-eat buffet from God's kitchen. All you have to do is open it up and dig in.

As the adage goes, "You are what you eat".

Therefore, you can only release what you have absorbed. If you are over-saturated with pop culture and human philosophy, that is all you can offer people. Essentially you become a reflection of the things you consume. To put it another way; what you consume – *consumes* you.

Think about the following questions and ask yourself if you're a sponge or a strainer:

- What kinds of music do you download? Of that music, what messages do you find in the lyrics?
- What were the last two books you read (not including this one)?
- Is there an actor, artist or athlete you admire? If so, what is it about them you find appealing or inspiring?
- Where do you get your sense of style and fashion?
- What were the last two movies you saw?
- In a week, how many hours do you think you spent surfing the web or on Facebook?
- If possible, think about the last couple of times you got together with your friends. What were your conversations about?

Maybe these questions seem silly or even an invasion of your privacy. Here's the reality. The answers may help explain why you think and act the way you do—right or wrong. Your thoughts, emotions and actions don't just fall from the sky.

They are the products of what you feed your heart and mind.

Imagine what your life would look like if you fed yourself spiritual food. If you eat the meat of God's Word, you will develop into a mature Christian. If all you eat is junk food (unhealthy stuff), you become a reflection of that.

Maybe you already know the truth, but are just not obeying it. We've all been guilty of that. But through God's grace, not mere human ability, we can grow in our obedience.

Love Constrains Us

Growing up in church, there were times when I got sick of hearing about hearing do's and don'ts. Wear this, don't wear that. Go here, don't go there. Listen to this, don't listen to that. I'm just being honest. I struggled with that, especially in high school when all I wanted was to fit in. At times I felt constrained and imprisoned from doing what I wanted to do. I didn't like rules. What 17-year-old does?

I used to say to myself, "When I get older, I'm going to do what I want. No one is going to tell me what to do." Thank God that didn't happen. Most of the people I know who ventured outside of rules and authority found nothing but regret and confusion.

When I got older I realized that rules were meant to protect me, not destroy me. Don't get me wrong. I fully reject legalism, which over-emphasizes rule-keeping and views adherence to religious laws as *the* means to salvation. We are taught in Ephesians 2:8-9, "For by grace you have been saved through faith, and that not of yourselves; *it is* the gift of God, not of works, lest anyone should boast." On the flip side, we're not saved *by* works, but saved *to* works. The mark of a true follower of Christ is discipline (self-denial) and good works.

I sense that some believers, young adults in particular, confuse legalism and obedience, or legalism and discipline. Simply because a Biblical statute is applied doesn't mean God or your spiritual overseers are enforcing legalism. I recommend you study the differences and understand what we sometimes mistakenly refer to as "legalism" is actually "love".

We hardly recognize the role that God's love plays in our obedience and discipline. We think love is all about warm feelings, Christian soft-rock music and no rules. But the Bible paints a different picture. 2 Corinthians 5:14-15 (ESV) says, "For the love of Christ controls us, because we have concluded this: that one has died for all, therefore all have died; and He died for all, that those who live might no longer live for themselves but for Him who for their sake died and was raised."

The concept in these verses is that the love of Christ is like a tidal wave. When a strong tide of water hits the land, it carries everything away by force. When we accept God's love, He overwhelms us, sweeps us away and literally compels us to live for Him.

God floods your life through love and constrains you to obey Him by faith. If a father holds his little child's hand when crossing the street, you wouldn't view it as dictating, but protecting. Even though the child's "liberty" to run ahead or play is restricted, it's clear the father loves his child enough to grip his hand and control how far he can walk.

Why? It's simple: cars are speeding by and could hit the child. What a tragedy that would be. God's constraining love works the same way.

My goal in this book is not to define specific standards or practices. Church disciplines should be discussed at your local Church and with your family. I'm not going to discuss particulars. I'm merely pointing to the heart of the matter, which is what Jesus said, "If you love Me, keep My commandants" (John 14:15). As you go into the world, into college, into your career and so forth, God's love requires discipline and obedience. The way the world is headed today, this principle just may save you from losing the things that matter most.

Shift Keys

1. Adjust your eyes – Maybe it's time for an "eye exam" with God's Word. Psalm 101:3 reads, "I will set nothing wicked before my eyes; I hate the work of those who fall away; It shall not cling to me." Discerning culture requires a spiritual and Biblical point of view. Be one step ahead of the devil by keeping your guard up and relying on the Holy Spirit.

2. Arm your soul – This battle is not physical, but spiritual. Ephesians 6:12-13 reveals, "For we do not wrestle against flesh and blood, but against principalities, against powers, against the rulers of the darkness of this age, against spiritual hosts of wickedness in the heavenly places. Therefore take up the whole armor of God, that you may be able to withstand in the evil day, and having done all, to stand." Living victoriously in our culture requires spiritual preparation…and it starts with prayer!

3. Assess your heart – Jeremiah 17:9 diagnoses the human heart and its motives: "The heart is deceitful above all things, and desperately wicked; who can know it?" Maybe you should spend less time listening to your heart, and more time tuning into God's heart.

4 | The Risk of Doing Right

Indifference to Integrity

Someone is watching you, and your character is center stage. Abraham Lincoln once said, "Character is like a tree and reputation like a shadow. The shadow is what we think of it; the tree is the real thing."

Nothing will remain in the minds of others more than your character, the real you. Character is what turns good people into great people, good speakers into great speakers, good leaders into great leaders. Character defines you. It gives you a priceless value, one that never fades.

Your skills and resolve may shape your potential, but it is your character that shapes your legacy.

For me, character is about *walking* the *talk*, or simply practicing what I preach. I have found that it is always easier to teach principles from behind a pulpit than it is to live them. As a speaker, I admit it's much simpler to preach about forgiveness and reconciliation than it is to demonstrate them. Walking out your words is not easy, but when you have character, you understand it's vital.

If you achieve great things without the core of character, you will find success to be short-lived. Without a moral foundation, efforts to succeed will be overshadowed by the temptation to compromise. A solid character will manifest unwavering convictions and beliefs. It will balance your appetite for success, giving you a compass for every decision you make.

Most often, the virtue of character isn't really noticed until it's tested. Character is exhibited through crisis and conflict. In other words, true character, or its lack of, always reveals itself when the heat is on.

Character Counts

Character is an invisible virtue with visible value. Character is not tangible or touchable, but it always materializes. It's something that exhibits itself—usually when you're not aware of it. Your character will never warn you and say, "Hey, be careful, someone's watching." It simply shows. While character is *developed* through difficulties, it is also *displayed* through difficulties. Like gold, it only reveals its purity when the heat is on.

Character must be seen as a discipline, not a gift. It's something you work on daily. I don't believe God hands out a "character anointing" or a "gift of character." Character is built with the bricks of morality and integrity. It comes through a process of learning, growing and understanding. Your gifts and talents will create opportunities. Your character will influence what you do when those opportunities arise. Your gifts and talents may birth a ministry. Your character will birth a legacy. This is how you will be remembered.

Take a moment to think of someone you greatly admire. It could be your father, mother, mentor or friend. Identify what you admire most about this person. Perhaps it's tough to pinpoint just one thing, but try to narrow it down. Now, let me ask you this question: Is the quality you admire most one that reflects accomplishments (i.e. occupation, hobbies, financial successes, etc.), or character traits (i.e. honest, caring, brave, etc.)? I'm willing to bet that what you most admire about this person is his or her character traits.

Character has nearly nothing to do with what you do and everything to do with who you are. Contrary to popular opinion, who you are, not what you do, is what people will admire about your life. And yet most people are busy working to be better at *things*. Carpenters want to be better at woodworking, athletes want to be better at playing, designers want to be better at designing and the list goes on. We spend so much effort improving what we do that we end up spending little effort improving who we are. And yet our greatest legacy is found in who we are.

"The integrity of the upright shall guide them: but the perverseness of transgressors shall destroy them" (Proverbs 11:3 KJV). Having good character is having integrity. Integrity is the desire to do what's moral or ethical even when it's tough. It's the risk of doing right.

Although character is an invisible virtue, most of its benefits will eventually materialize. The fruit of your character will ripen, offering a sweet taste to everyone you influence. Character fruits include honesty, humility, unselfishness, morality, love and forgiveness. There are more fruits, but the underlying theme of them all is that character gives you moral authority and honor.

Maybe you're saying, "That sounds good, but how do I cultivate my character?" Here are a few suggestions:

1. Follow Jesus' example

While others base their character on good and moral things, as Christians we must base our character on Christ. In Christ we discover all that is holy, moral, just, righteous and pure. By learning and applying the traits of Christ, our character will grow in beautiful ways. Read the gospels of Matthew, Mark, Luke and John. Study how Jesus conducted Himself.

Observe how Jesus handled hot topics and sticky situations. Pay close attention to how He dealt with people's attitudes and skirmishes. Study His teachings. Read until you get a view of His heart. Consider how He responded to criticism, judgment, dishonesty, deception and cruelty. In other words, get to know Christ and you'll know character. By drawing from His example, you will understand what good character is. Jesus is the ultimate template for character.

2. Obtain Godly wisdom

God's word tells us, "Trust in the LORD with all your heart, and lean not on your own understanding; in all your ways acknowledge Him, and He shall direct your paths" (Proverbs 3:5-6). The fast lane to poor character is refusing counsel. Those who feel they know everything are sure to be trapped by something.

Man's own wisdom is frail and at times misguided, but God's wisdom is potent and life-changing. Should you ever have doubts, don't be afraid to ask for help. Talk to your leader, your mentor, preferably someone older and more experienced.

Cultivating your character involves a process of obtaining Godly wisdom for daily decisions. Some of the greatest men and women of character are those who weren't too proud to stop and ask for directions.

Maybe it's a guy thing, but I don't like pulling over and asking for directions. Admitting that I don't know where I'm headed is humbling. I'd rather miss a couple of turns than to ask some gas station clerk. I know—it's a bit ridiculous. However, when it comes to decisions and choices that affect my family, my reputation or my ministry, I must pull over and ask for counsel. And hopefully friends will hold me accountable.

Proverbs 20:5 states, "Counsel in the heart of man is like deep water, but a man of understanding will draw it out". We all need to drop our water pots into the depth of Godly counsel so that our character will be strengthened. God's wisdom is available. All you have to do is ask.

3. Examine yourself regularly

Don't be afraid to look at your life in the mirror. The person who refuses to examine himself is not willing to face or deal with reality. We often fear the mirror of introspection because we're afraid of what we might see. If we are to mature in our character, we must be willing to deal with unhealthy attributes and traits.

Simply ignoring a matter doesn't erase it. It is crucial for you to understand that the strength of your in-look determines the power of your outlook. Someone who doesn't recognize personal error, immaturity or mistakes and doesn't try to improve is someone whose character is shallow.

I'm reminded of the time that David cried these words, "Search me, O God, and know my heart: try me, and know my thoughts: And see if there be any wicked way in me, and lead me in the way everlasting" (Psalm 139:23-24, KJV). Self-examination isn't for those who presume failure—it's for those who pursue success. If you aren't already practicing this, begin today. Through prayer, ask God to show you areas in your life that need improvement. Then ask Him to help you fortify your character. Gradually you'll begin to notice a change.

Character Costs

Character is doing the right thing, no matter what cost or risk is involved.

When you were a child, did telling a lie sometimes seem like the easiest path to take? If you broke your mother's favorite vase, denying guilt might have felt better at the moment, but eventually your lie probably would have caught up to you. Then, instead of being punished just for breaking the vase, you were punished for lying too. Practicing integrity may have its initial sting, but doing the right thing always pays off in the long run.

Joseph's encounter with Potiphar's wife is a powerful illustration of being willing to suffer for doing the right thing. As a young man, Joseph was seduced by his master's wife, but he stood firm against her wiles. When Potiphar's wife sashayed around Joseph with her batting eyelashes and scented fragrance, his character was being tested. Day after day, she tried to seduce Joseph and lure him into her bedroom. Yet every time she would pressure him, he refused.

A man with no integrity or moral character might have consented, but because Joseph was a Godly, moral man, he continued to resist her flirtatious appeals. The result: he was falsely accused, demoted and imprisoned. Let's read the story:

"She kept putting pressure on him day after day, but he refused to sleep with her, and he kept out of her way as much as possible. One day, however, no one else was around when he was doing his work inside the house. She came and grabbed him by his shirt, demanding, "Sleep with me!" Joseph tore himself away, but as he did, his shirt came off. She was left holding it as he ran from the house. When she saw that she had his shirt and that he had fled, she began screaming. Soon all the men around the place came running. "My husband has brought this Hebrew slave here to insult us!" she sobbed. "He tried to rape me, but I screamed. When he heard my loud cries, he ran and left his shirt behind with me." She kept the shirt with her, and when her husband came home that night, she told him her story. "That Hebrew slave you've had around here tried to make a fool of me," she said. "I was saved only by my screams. He ran out, leaving his shirt behind!" After hearing his wife's story, Potiphar was furious! He took Joseph and threw him into the prison where the king's prisoners were held" (Genesis 39:10-20, NLT).

How can this be?

How could a man who did the right thing be treated this way?

Joseph's immediate compensation for righteousness was a prison sentence. In his case, displaying character was costly. Doing the honorable thing cost Joseph his freedom.

We will all encounter a "Potiphar's wife" sooner or later. Potiphar's wife represents temptation, seducing spirits, sin and immorality. Your Potiphar's wife may not be a sensual matter, but perhaps a business or ministry choice. She could present herself in various ways. Her batting eyelashes might be the lust for financial gain. Her overpowering fragrance might be the enticement of personal pleasure. Whatever form Potiphar's wife takes in your life, resist. At all costs, resist. If it means demotion and denial, resist. If it means a prison of suffering is to be your new home, continue to resist. The long-term reward will be more than worth the cost.

Finding Favor with God

Character always prevails. Potiphar's wife probably presumed that Joseph was finished; however, it was quite the opposite. God is more concerned about holiness and character than gifts, talents, anointing or position. He gives favor to the upright.

Here's what happened next: "But the LORD was with Joseph there, too, and He granted Joseph favor with the chief jailer. Before long, the jailer put Joseph in charge of all the other prisoners and over everything that happened in the prison. The chief jailer had no more worries after that, because Joseph took care of everything. The LORD was with him, making everything run smoothly and successfully" (Genesis 39:21-23, NLT).

The key to God's favor is resisting sin and standing for what's right. Sure, Joseph suffered a little bit, but his suffering wasn't in vain. While hidden in the prison, the Lord was with him.

I love the way the verse following Joseph's imprisonment begins with, "But the LORD was with Joseph there, too." Satan, the jokes on you!

God abides near those who uphold morality and holiness. While sleeping behind prison walls, God was with him. I'd rather be imprisoned with God than free to walk without Him. Character costs—but its benefits always pay off. You might not see the results of the decisions and choices you're making right now for ten to fifteen years, or maybe not even this side of heaven. But know that choosing God's way is right and pleases your Father and opens the door to His blessings.

Godly character will help you make the right choices. Joseph was anointed, gifted and chosen, but without the character to make the right choices, his destiny would have been canceled.

To ensure God's favor upon your life, grow in character and God will bless your path.

Shift Keys

1. Talk to God daily – Character is sculpted by the hands of God. That process is realized through a daily conversation called *prayer*. God authored morality and imprinted a conscience into every human. He is the authority and expert on the subjects of integrity and holiness. It's the very essence of who God is. If you're going to grow in character, you must continue to meet God in the secret place of prayer.

2. Be honest about your struggles – Character is about authenticity, about being honest and transparent. If you can't be honest with yourself or with others about your struggles or weaknesses, they will eventually destroy you. Hiding your sins or struggles will also lead to a double life, one that allows you to create false versions of yourself. That's a dangerous place to be. Always be honest and truthful.

3. Recognize your worth – I believe that our behavior is often a reflection of how we see ourselves. Know that you are God's beloved child, that you are valuable. Your character should flow from an awareness of God's favor on your life. Knowing your worth will determine what kind of choices you make.

Part 2: Inward Shifts

5 | When Life Goes Dark
Depressed to Delivered

Depression. It's a real problem. Maybe you're one of the millions of young adults who live in the darkness of depression. In this chapter, I want to help you understand what depression is, what it looks like and how to defeat it. In order to enjoy life and fulfill God's purpose, you have to be set free from this vicious cycle of gloom. For the purpose of this chapter, I will be presenting some symptoms of depression; however, my intention is not to clinically diagnose a condition, but simply to provide awareness and insight.

Many of us at different points in life get depressed. Of course, not all of us *stay* depressed and we all don't experience the same degree of depression. But there's no denying that depression among American young adults is on the rise and reaching record levels.

For a young Christian, depression can be a serious problem.

Why, you might ask? Well, because you're a "young Christian". Allow me to explain.

First, let's consider your stage of life. That alone is a tough process. It's not unusual for young adults to feel "down in the dumps" occasionally. Life is changing rapidly. Academically and socially, you're experiencing new pressures and expectations. Life is starting to seem more unfair and when things go wrong, it feels like the end of the world. Here are just a few probing questions:

Do you often feel like things don't go your way?

Do you overreact to small disappointments?

Do higher demands at school or work stress you out?

If so, that doesn't make you depressed. It just makes you normal. It's normal to feel this way in your young adult life. You're still adjusting to expectations that for the majority of your life you haven't had to worry about. It's important to recognize these changes because when you experience significant pain or loss (separate from the normal stuff), it can snowball into a real state of depression.

Second, there is the fact that you are a Christian and in the minds of many people, Christians supposed to be 100% happy all the time. We falsely believe that if we're depressed, then maybe we're suffering from a spiritual malfunction or that God is shaking His head in disapproval. This sort of logic leads to destructive thoughts. Here are a few:

- If I'm supposed to be able to heal the sick, why can't I remove these thoughts from my mind?

- If Jesus promised an abundant life, why do I feel so melancholy and defeated?

- Maybe I haven't fully surrendered my life to Jesus.

- I feel like such a failure.

"Depressed Christian" seems like an oxymoron. And for that reason, depression carries extra baggage in a believer's life. On top of being depressed, now you feel guilty and ashamed because of it. Instead of letting yourself down, or your family down, now you feel like you're letting God down. Then perhaps some misguided people accuse you of hiding a sin or being a rebel.

Other well-meaning believers might tell you, "just get over it" or "just have faith". After statements like these, you end up feeling more guilty and rejected. Although spiritual problems—like habitual sin, doubt, or spiritual attack—certainly can cause depression, those things are often the result of depression, not the cause.

Unmasking Depression

If you Google the word "depression" you'll find an endless sea of resources, definitions and organizations who devote themselves to fighting it. Major studies have been conducted and published over the years that drive awareness and educate our society about depression and its symptoms.

According to the A.D.A.M. Medical Encyclopedia, "Depression may be described as feeling sad, blue, unhappy, miserable, or down in the dumps. Most of us feel this way at one time or another for short periods. True clinical depression is a mood disorder in which feelings of sadness, loss, anger, or frustration interfere with everyday life for weeks or longer."[4]

If the definition of depression doesn't resonate very much with you, maybe the statistics will. You may be alarmed at how prevalent depression and suicide has become, especially among young adults.

- Among adolescents 12 to 17 years old in California, 8% suffered an episode of major depression from 2008 – 2009.[5]

---

[4] A.D.A.M. Medical Encyclopedia [Internet]. Atlanta (GA): A.D.A.M., Inc.; c1997-2011. Asthma; [last reviewed 2012 Mar 7; cited 2012 Nov 2]. Available from: http://www.ncbi.nlm.nih.gov/pubmedhealth/PMH0001941/
[5] National Survey on Drug Use and Health, 2008-2009

- Suicide is the third leading cause of death for 15-to-24-year-olds.[6]

- 44% of American college students reported feeling symptoms of depression.[7]

- 30% of American college students reported feeling "so depressed that it was difficult to function".[8]

Depression left untreated or unhealed can cause serious problems in your health and relationships. It can also lead you to drug addiction, alcoholism and immoral sexual activity. And as indicated above, suicide is the leading cause of death for young adults.

Even young Christians find themselves battling suicidal thoughts. In the last several years, I've sat and counseled with young men and women who cut themselves because they don't know how to cope with emotional hurt or abuse. I've listened to young men confess that they have attempted suicide and struggle with those thoughts.

The Symptoms:

---

[6] American Academy of Child and Adolescent Psychiatry, 2008

[7] Borchard, T. (2010). Statistics About College Depression. *Psych Central.* Retrieved on November 2, 2012, from
http://psychcentral.com/blog/archives/2010/09/02/statistics-about-college-depression/

[8] American College Health Association. *American College Health Association-National College Health Assessment II: Reference Group Executive Summary Fall 2009.* Linthicum, MD: American College Health Association; 2009.

Now that I've defined depression to some degree, it's important to recognize the symptoms. As I alluded earlier, depression is not easily detected in young adults, because it's often assumed that certain behavior or mood swings are typical. But there are ways to detect depression in yourself and in your friends. Below are some symptoms you shouldn't ignore:

- Persistent sad or anxious mood
- Anger, restlessness, irritability
- Sleeplessness, or not enough sleep
- Reduced appetite and weight loss, or increased appetite and weight gain
- Loss of pleasure and interest in things once enjoyed
- Persistent physical symptoms that don't respond to treatment (such as chronic pain or digestive disorders)
- Difficulty concentrating, remembering or making decisions
- Fatigue or loss of energy
- Feeling guilty, hopeless or worthless
- Thoughts of suicide or death

The Triggers:

Any one or a combination of things can trigger depression, including:

- Death or serious illness of a friend or family member
- Loss of love or attention from a friend or family member
- Breakup of a romantic relationship
- Family problems, especially parents' divorce
- Isolation/loneliness
- Rejection or bullying
- Physical, verbal, and/or sexual abuse
- Unplanned pregnancy
- Chemical imbalance
- Hormonal changes, including PMS
- Substance abuse
- Hospitalization, especially for a chronic illness

Denying the existence or prevalence of depression is simply unacceptable. Everyone has to take responsibility and have this conversation at the appropriate time. In this chapter I will provide biblical steps towards healing and freedom. But first I want to issue a word of caution about how we view depression.

Word of Caution:

Christians are sometimes afraid to admit that depression *can* be a disease, believing that *most* if not *all* cases are spiritually triggered and therefore must be remedied spiritually. *Clinical depression*, however, is a physical condition that must be diagnosed by a physician. In some cases, depression can be caused by a physical disorder that needs to be treated with medication and/or counseling.

God is able to cure any disease, illness or disorder. Nothing is impossible for Him. However, let us use wisdom. Sometimes, seeing a doctor for depression is no different than seeing a doctor for an injury or physical disease. Deciding to see a doctor would be a personal decision, or between you and your family or trusted advisor.

Jesus: Man of Sorrows

Our comfort and hope is that Jesus came to deliver us from the clutches of sin and shame. Through Jesus and His Cross, every curse against us is smashed. He is our Savior! And central to the Gospel is that Jesus not only saved us, but became *like* us. Half the battle is won just knowing that Jesus understands what you're feeling and going through.

The Bible never explicitly says that Jesus was depressed, but He faced extreme pressure from both political and religious opponents. In the hours leading up to His death, Jesus was left alone, deserted by His closest friends and denied by His closest followers.

In the garden of Gethsemane, Jesus was under such extreme stress and grief that blood dripped as sweat from His brow. He was falsely accused, brought before a mock trial and was sentenced to the most horrific death imaginable. After being cursed at, spat upon, lacerated with whips and crowned with razor-sharp thorns, His hands and feet were nailed to a rugged cross.

As Jesus' naked, bloody body was hoisted and pinned up on the cross, He felt the utter shame and disgust of humanity. He hung as a symbol of ultimate rejection and repulsion. The most innocent man who ever lived was crucified without any due process or a fair trial.

If you have ever wondered if Jesus knows what you are going through, He does. Hebrews 4:14-16 reassures us:

"Seeing then that we have a great High Priest who has passed through the heavens, Jesus the Son of God, let us hold fast our confession. For we do not have a High Priest who cannot sympathize with our weaknesses, but was in all points tempted as we are, yet without sin. Let us therefore come boldly to the throne of grace, that we may obtain mercy and find grace to help in time of need."

When God became man, it allowed Him to experience humanity in the truest sense. Jesus can relate to what you are going through, even depression. This is a factual statement because Scripture affirms the full humanity of Jesus Christ.

Jesus Christ is God manifested in the flesh (Ref. 1 Tim. 3:16). Jesus was not an earthly hologram or heavenly flesh. Jesus was not God's avatar or remote-controlled human. Jesus was not immune from suffering and pain. The prophet Isaiah foretold: "He is despised and rejected by men, a Man of sorrows and acquainted with grief..." (Isaiah 53:3).

If your perception of Jesus is that He cares, but doesn't *really* know how you feel, that can become the main reason why you're not overcoming depression. But, Jesus was a man "acquainted with grief". If anyone knows how you feel, Jesus knows. That's why you can approach Him with confidence, knowing that He didn't read about depression or emotional pain in a book. Jesus lived through it so you wouldn't have to.

Isaiah also wrote, "Surely He has borne our griefs and carried our sorrows..." (Isaiah 53:4). Maybe you need to read that verse again. If you miss this point, then you will fail to see that dark sorrows belong to Jesus and not you.

The darkest area of your life, in your heart, belongs to Jesus.

Jesus carries *our* sorrows, *our* heartaches, *our* hurts. Jesus is not the Man of Sorrows because He was melancholy, had a broken childhood or a tattered past. He's the Man of Sorrows because He took our sorrows and sins upon Himself. On the cross, Jesus absorbed every sin, disease and curse that destroys human life.

You don't have to accept depression and live a repressive life. Jesus Christ died on the cross and shed His precious blood so that you could live in total victory. The power the Gospel is that through Jesus Christ, we are set free from guilt and shame.

Depression won't leave merely by thinking positive thoughts or through human will power. The Gospel is the ultimate remedy against destructive emotions of any kind.

Know the Truth

Besides the "shift" key, another key on the keyboard that is equally important is the "delete" key. It's the one key that has power to erase or eliminate. As a writer, I use the delete key to remove words or whole sentences. Sometimes we have to delete files on our hard drives that have been corrupted or contain a virus.

The same goes for life.

Through Jesus Christ, we have the power to delete depression and other destructive emotions and thoughts. But how is this accomplished? Is there an actual button you can press? Or is there some kind of spiritual wand that you can wave around? What's the secret to living a victorious life and deleting depression?

Here's the delete key: Know the *truth*.

Jesus declared: "And you shall know the truth, and the truth shall make you free" (John 8:32).

Victory hinges on what you choose to believe. Let me share a secret with you: how you feel is a product of what you believe. If you believe something to be true (even if it's false), it shapes your perception. It could be that most of your beliefs about yourself are rooted in lies or years of brainwashing.

Therefore, what you need is an encounter with Truth. Jesus said, "I am the way, the truth and the life. No one comes to the Father except through Me" (John 14:6). Truth is not necessarily a concept or philosophy. Truth is not an abstract idea or personal opinion. And it's certainly not the offspring of human wisdom and intellect. Truth is a Man named Jesus Christ. Jesus *is* truth.

Truth is liberating. Ignorance is incarcerating.

If there's one point I want to drill down, is that what you feel or experience, be it depression, fear or bitterness, doesn't change who God is. God is not defined by our feelings. Just because you don't feel His love, doesn't mean that God isn't love. God is love, not because you feel His love, but because that's what His Word says.

If you feel rejected or forgotten, that doesn't cancel God's Word which affirms that through Christ we are accepted and beloved. Your feelings or experiences do not define God. Consequently, your feelings shouldn't define or change you who are either. If you feel depressed, that doesn't disvalue you as an individual. You don't have to embrace that label and live like a victim. You don't have to be a drama-magnet just because you experience some gloom.

You can wave goodbye to depression simply by hiding out with Jesus. Declare to God, "You are my hiding place; You shall preserve me from trouble; You shall surround me with songs of deliverance" (Psalm 32:7). Embrace the finished work of Jesus Christ who died on the cross and rose again three days later. He conquered hell, death and the grave. He *killed* death and brought *fear* to fear. He overcame the world.

Stop trying to be your own hero. Let Jesus be your hero. Let Him be your champion, your counselor, your medicine and your friend.

Shift Keys

1. Enlighten yourself – This chapter was written partly to drive awareness about depression and its side-effects on young adults. Depression is real and should not be distorted by cultural or religious misconceptions. We should not be afraid to talk about it. If you're a ministry leader, it would be beneficial to enlighten yourself on depression and how to help young adults who battle it.

2. Relate to Jesus – We have a God who can relate to us in every sense. That's pretty amazing if you think about it. We can't imagine the physical and emotional pain that Jesus endured on our behalf. As He hung on the cross, tears mixed with blood, He felt totally abandoned by everybody. Depression would be an understatement.

3. Tell the Truth – Jesus called Satan "the father of lies" (Ref. John 8:44), revealing the origin of all lies—whether spoken by Satan or by humans. Deception is whenever a lie is believed or perceived as truth. That's the false world Satan wants Christians to live in. Accept nothing but the truth – expressed by Jesus Christ and written in the Word of God. Depression is defeated at the cross and you are a child of God!

6 | The Gift that Keeps Forgiving

Bitter to Better

Life hurts. On second thought, *people* hurt. Sure, life in general can be unfair and difficult. But let's face it; most of our disappointments in life come from people who either let us down or deliberately hurt us. And contrary to what we said as kids, words do hurt more than sticks and stones. Since we live in a fallen world populated with flawed people, the chances of you being offended and hurt by someone is highly probable.

Although I have no proof, right now there's at least a 50% chance you are offended, hurt or embittered by someone. I actually think my percentage is modest because I think most people who are bitter try to hide it – especially those with tough personalities and those who struggle to admit their weaknesses.

This book wouldn't be complete without a chapter about forgiveness. It's a reality that everyone has or will face in this life. If you can learn how to deal with offenses in a healthy manner, you will avoid the curse of living with resentment.

Whenever I preach about forgiveness, the mood in the church always seems to change. It's like if someone turned on the heater and closed the windows – in the middle of August. Most pastors are able to discern the tension that rises when Scripture confronts our human tendencies and sins. When forgiveness is the topic of conversation or teaching, people who are offended either confess or conceal. Those who conceal have either given up hope or have convinced themselves that nothing is wrong – basically living in denial.

Perhaps most people evade the road to forgiveness because they're afraid of what they'll discover about themselves. The last thing a victim wants to admit is that he played a part, or somehow implicated himself. For that reason, healing can become a tricky process because it requires total honesty and responsibility.

On the other hand, there are many innocent victims of cruelty in cases of abuse or injustice. For those individuals, forgiveness is often unimaginable and sends the wrong message. In these cases, forgiveness feels like you're agreeing with the offense or offender and says that what was done is "okay". Basically, it feels like you lost the battle or quit.

In this chapter, we're going to explore how offenses evolve, and then how to overcome through forgiveness. We often start these conversations by discussing bitterness. But truthfully, bitterness is the final stage of an offense. The Bible describes bitterness as a "root", and if you've ever done some yard work, you know that roots are not easy to remove.

The Evolution of Bitterness

Satan's agenda is to perpetuate ignorance. If he can keep you in the dark, then he can keep you in bondage. But the Holy Spirit illuminates truth. This isn't merely psychological warfare; this is spiritual warfare. Every action or thought you carry out should be guided by the Holy Spirit and based on the Word of God. Otherwise you're only shadow boxing and not actually punching out the problem.

Let's see how bitterness evolves and how to prevent its roots from deepening in your life.

1. Wrong produces Hurt

Hurts happen when someone directly or indirectly wrongs you. The wrong can be verbal, physical or even psychological in nature. It's safe to say we have all been wronged at one point or another. No one is exempt because, again, we live in a fallen world populated with flawed people. Wrongs will happen on a daily basis. The nature of the wrong will vary from circumstance to circumstance. The level of hurt will vary from person to person, based on how severe the wrong was and what provoked it.

It helps to remember that injustice is not only a product of this fallen world, but is often engineered by Satan – the accuser of the brethren (Rev. 12:10). But we are reminded in Isaiah 54:17 that, "No weapon formed against you shall prosper..." Whenever you're wronged, keep that scripture in mind. It doesn't mean that weapons won't form. They *will* form against you. But they *won't* prosper because you're a child of the living God.

2. Hurt produces Anger

If a hurt isn't healed properly, it will lead to anger and vengeance. Anger isn't necessarily a sin. Sometimes it's the appropriate response. God's grace allows us to be angry for a period of time, but eventually that anger has to convert into something constructive.

Ephesians 4:26 crystalizes this point: "Be angry, and do not sin: do not let the sun go down on your wrath." I'll be the first to admit, this is easier said than done. But when anger festers, we quickly start to justify our retaliation. The Bible reminds us that it's not our job to settle the score. Romans 12:19 states,

"Beloved, do not avenge yourselves, but rather give place to wrath; for it is written, "Vengeance is Mine, I will repay," says the Lord."

3. Anger produces Bitterness

If anger consumes the heart, it will eventually germinate into a root of bitterness. This is when you permanently accommodate your hurts. At this point, people generally stop sympathizing with you and expect you to find closure and move on with your life. Friends and family won't come around as often because your personality is soured with negativity. Cynicism will begin to taint your perspective of life and even God. Eventually, you blame everyone who doesn't agree with you. You can try to cover your bitterness with deceitful acts of diplomacy, but in the end you won't feel any better about yourself. Your blame games will corner you into a stalemate situation where nobody wins.

The moment you perceive that the other side is winning or you feel threatened, you'll try to manipulate family members and friends by maintaining the status of a victim. You may even attempt to manipulate Scriptures and God's Name in order to rationalize your bitterness or convince neutral parties to join your side.

Sadly, you'll get to the point where you don't even like yourself. Regardless of who was originally right or wrong, your hatred will invert until you can't stand your own reflection. Bitter people usually end up bitter with themselves more than anyone else. You become your worst enemy.

Let me take it a step further. Your injury can become your idol. You listen to it. You cradle it. You enshrine it and see the world through it. You bow to its demands. You let it define your mood.

Read the following lines carefully. Any ministry conceived in anger or hurt will either be stillborn or self-detonate with vanity (e.g. David's son Absalom). Since victims need attention, your ministry will end up being a public therapy session where you are either the star attraction that needs praise, or a voluntary scapegoat that needs pity. Ministering "through" pain is different than ministering "for" pain. Therefore, allow God's grace to hide you, heal you and help you forgive.

If you're bitter, you cannot enjoy God's blessings because you won't allow yourself to. You won't embrace new things because your mind will always rehearse the past. You won't welcome new relationships because you'll be afraid that this new person might do you wrong like others have. You won't trust God to the fullest because part of you will blame God for what happened, or feel that God is punishing you for not trying harder.

If you're bitter, you won't love serving people because you'll feel that others owe you an apology and should actually be serving you instead. You'll struggle to give because you'll always be the one taking. If you're bitter, you won't be happy because you keep defining happiness based on how you feel from day to day, instead of by God's grace and love.

I once saw a quote that read, "Bitterness is letting someone live rent-free in your head". Well, if that's the case, I say it's time to evict that emotion and change the locks!

Root of the Problem

I don't like yard work, but as a kid I didn't have a choice. When my dad asked my brothers and I to put on work clothes and help him in the yard, there wasn't an option to say "no" or "I'm busy".

Some jobs were not as bad, like clipping a few overgrown branches. But my nemesis was pulling weeds. It's probably what makes me hate yard work to this day. The first few times I removed weeds, I made the mistake of chopping them at the surface level only. For a moment it all seemed good as I was ready to pat myself on the back. But then my dad finally saw what I was doing and told me that unless I pull out the root of the weed, it's going to grow back.

He was right. Just a few days later, you could see little weeds shooting up from the ground.

As much as I despise yard work, it did show me this important lesson about life: *Wounds cannot be healed on the surface.* In order to experience real freedom from emotional pain like bitterness, it has to be confronted on the deepest level—otherwise it will resurface with time. For example, switching churches because another member offended you may solve the immediate issue. You will certainly enjoy momentary relief from having to interact with that individual, but your inability to forgive will continue to affect how you live.

Once I grew up and got married, I thought my yard work days were behind me and I could retire my shovel and rake. But when we purchased our first townhome, I suddenly had to face my old nemesis. Our home had a small garden next to our porch and a larger one in the back patio. It didn't take long for those pesky weeds to sprout up. It was like they all ganged up on me.

Thank God for weed killer. But even then, some of the larger weeds still needed to be pulled out by hand.

Bitterness is a root, not a symptom. It hides just beneath the surface. Hebrews 12:15 illustrates this principle: "looking carefully lest anyone fall short of the grace of God; lest any root of bitterness springing up cause trouble, and by this many become defiled". Let's unpack this text by asking what roots and bitterness have in common? I came up with three similarities:

1. Grows beneath the surface

Roots are not visible to the eye because they grow underground. The same is true about bitterness, because it can fester under the radar for years. You can mask your true feelings and be secretly bitter without anyone else knowing it. This component of bitterness is what makes it a silent killer.

2. Springs up on the outside

Roots are designed to eventually sprout above the surface in the form of plants, flowers, trees and of course—weeds. If you harbor bitterness, you can only hide it for so long. Eventually, your emotions will manifest themselves in some form of behavior, attitude or demeanor. Bitterness will pollute every area of your life. It will surface in your relationships, academics and spiritual devotions.

3. Resurfaces unless it's uprooted

Like those annoying weeds, trying to clean up the surface with emotional highs, periods of happiness or other distractions (i.e. sports, entertainment and material things) will not solve the root problem. This method of coping will create a false reality built on denial and fear. After the high or fix wears off, your pain or anger will show up again without warning.

If you've been hiding your bitterness, are you tired of pretending to be well, when really your heart is sick? Are you fed up with the drama of awkward feelings and tension when you see that person who hurt you? Are you ready to get beyond the anger, the hatred and the resentment?

When your heart is sour with bitterness, it denies you the abundant life that Jesus Christ promised. It forces you into a lifestyle of self-pity and victimhood, where Satan loves to twist reality. But there is tangible hope in the power of the Gospel, because when Jesus Christ died on the cross and rose again, He conquered every sin, dysfunction and disease (physical and emotional) including death itself.

How does the Gospel empower you to uproot bitterness from your heart?

The answer is found in one word.

Forgive.

Forgiven to Forgive

Over the last ten years, I've probably devoted more time to writing about forgiveness than any other topic. My first book, *The Woman's Touch,* explained the need for forgiveness and through God's grace, brought healing to many hurting women.

In fact, all five of my previous books contain insights on forgiveness. It's been a recurring theme in my ministry. I say that not to boast, but to admit that I'm still learning about forgiveness. And quite honestly, I'm still learning how to forgive.

I can assure you that with age comes perspective. With each stage of life, I see forgiveness from a different angle.

Forgiveness is an issue that every human faces. One of the 7 billion people in the world is bound to hurt you—once, twice, well…quite a few times as long as you're alive. So it's in your best interest to understand why forgiveness matters so much to God and what kind of impact it has on society.

I usually approach the issue of forgiveness by telling a story from the Bible. As I'm writing this, a bunch of stories come to mind – Joseph and his brothers, Jacob and Esau, the Prodigal Son, Jesus and the adulteress woman – just to name a few. All of them merit our study. However, the imagery in Jesus' parable of the unforgiving servant paints a picture of a divine reality that often gets whitewashed. Rather than appeal to your emotions, I'm compelled to share direct truth concerning this matter.

This parable was a response to Peter's question in Matthew 18:21, "Lord, how often shall my brother sin against me, and I forgive him? Up to seven times?" It was a fair question. But it was also a little self-serving. Regardless, Jesus blew their minds when He answered, "I do not say to you, up to seven times, but up to seventy times seven". Jesus wasn't saying to forgive 490 times (7 x 70). The point is that we should forgive an infinite number of times. In other words, stop counting and just do it.

The parable is found in Matthew 18:23-35:

"Therefore the kingdom of heaven is like a certain king who wanted to settle accounts with his servants. And when he had begun to settle accounts, one was brought to him who owed him ten thousand talents. But as he was not able to pay, his master commanded that he be sold, with his wife and children and all that he had, and that payment be made. The servant therefore fell down before him, saying, 'Master, have patience with me, and I will pay you all.' Then the master of that servant was moved with compassion, released him, and forgave him the debt.

"But that servant went out and found one of his fellow servants who owed him a hundred denarii; and he laid hands on him and took *him* by the throat, saying, 'Pay me what you owe!' So his fellow servant fell down at his feet and begged him, saying, 'Have patience with me, and I will pay you all.' And he would not, but went and threw him into prison till he should pay the debt. So when his fellow servants saw what had been done, they were very grieved, and came and told their master all that had been done. Then his master, after he had called him, said to him, 'You wicked servant! I forgave you all that debt because you begged me. Should you not also have had compassion on your fellow servant, just as I had pity on you?' And his master was angry, and delivered him to the torturers until he should pay all that was due to him.

"So My heavenly Father also will do to you if each of you, from his heart, does not forgive his brother his trespasses."

Here's the plot in four scenes:

Scene 1: A servant owed a king a large sum of money that he couldn't afford to pay. The servant begged for mercy. The king felt compassion and forgave his debt.

Scene 2: The forgiven servant had a fellow servant who owed him a small amount of money. The forgiven servant choked him and demanded the payment. The other servant begged for mercy.

Scene 3: The forgiven servant had no mercy, but threw him into prison until the debt was paid. Ironically, the servant was put in a situation where he could never repay.

Scene 4: The king heard of the forgiven servant's ungrateful refusal to forgive another servant's debt. The king then sentenced the unmerciful servant to be jailed and tortured until he could repay the full amount—the same situation as the other servant.

The message in this parable is simple: *if you don't forgive, you won't be forgiven.*

Jesus reinforced this truth in Matthew 6:15: "But if you do not forgive men their trespasses, neither will your Father forgive your trespasses."

Ouch.

It ruffles my feathers a little and I'm the one who typed it. But here's the thing. It really doesn't matter how we feel about it. It's the cold truth. We simply have to wrestle with it until it transforms us. Jesus is not going to make exceptions, no matter how bad you've been hurt or mistreated. Why, you ask? It's a matter of principle, not feelings. The principle is that if Jesus Christ has forgiven us and cleared our debt of sin, then He expects us to forgive others just the same.

I can't possibly tell you how many times I've been the ungrateful servant who quickly forgets just how forgiven he is. I've been hurt by people (friends and family) on quite a few occasions, but that doesn't thwart God's command.

In His model prayer, Jesus said, "And forgive us our debts, as we forgive our debtors" (Matt. 6:12). Notice the comma between the two phrases—implying that this is one truth, not two separate concepts. The first phrase "forgive us our debts" is entirely contingent on the second, "as we forgive our debtors". Yet there is a tendency to gloss over the second part or obey only when it's rational.

People say things like, "but you don't know what he did" or "she doesn't deserve to be forgiven". Clearly, it's hard to argue against such emotions. How can anyone deny you your right to feel what you feel? This is why Jesus had to use such strong imagery and bold black-and-white statements. He knew that most times, there is no human rationale for forgiving someone. We simply must forgive because we're forgiven and want to cherish His grace.

God's forgiveness is the gift that keeps on forgiving.

God's Word assures us that He is faithful to forgive our sins and cleanse us from all unrighteousness (See 1 John 1:9). Therefore, let's practice this and begin to uproot bitterness, resentment and malice in our hearts. I don't have a magic formula or a wand to make the act of forgiveness any easier. But let us find ourselves at the rugged cross where Jesus was crucified, murdered for our debts, and yet cried out, "Father forgive them, for they know not what they do".

Shift Keys

1. Check your heart – Are you holding a grudge against someone? Instead of trying to convince yourself that you're not offended or that you've got it under control, it's better to admit you're offended and forgive. If you don't get honest about your true feelings, bitterness will take root and pollute every area of your life.

2. Forgive and let go – Simply "praying away the hurt" isn't going to work unless it's attached to genuine forgiveness. Others feel that time heals all wounds. The reality is that time only deepens our wounds. As hard as it may seem, you must forgive and let go in order to experience freedom and enjoy God's blessings.

3. Give what you receive – God's forgiveness of our sins was a gift. We did absolutely nothing to earn that gift. It was simply given to us freely, by God's grace, and through the death of Jesus on the Cross. Putting all emotions aside, it's not up to us to decide who gets forgiven and who doesn't. God is the judge, not us. Jesus reminds us, "But if you do not forgive men their trespasses, neither will your Father forgive your trespasses."

7 | Scar Wars

Hurt to Healed

A couple of years ago I was preaching at a youth conference in Northern California. My message was about spiritual warfare. I'll admit; I wasn't exactly hitting a home run. The air was thick and at one point I wondered if my message was too heavy for the crowd. As I wrapped up my sermon, I was ready to strike up the band and bail out my sermon with a song.

But then something happened. The Holy Spirit prompted me to make a special invitation to young adults who were feeling depressed, suicidal or emotionally imprisoned. My first reaction was, "Lord, are you sure? These are *church* kids—Christians. They don't have those kinds of deep issues or scars."

I know. It was wrong of me to question God. But I honestly didn't think many, if any, would come forward. So I did a "here goes nothing...we'll see what happens" altar call. After making the call, I put my head down and just hoped that at least one person would come up so I wouldn't look like a rookie preacher.

After hearing what sounded like people standing up and walking, I lifted up my head and opened my eyes. What I saw was a large group of young adults, many of whom began to weep and plant their faces into their hands, as if to hide in shame.

God's power was present to deliver and heal, and many young adults were set free that night.

After this experience, I wondered how these young adults coped with their hurts and scars before this night of deliverance. That question has continued to burden me. If you're a young adult who's been wounded in any way, know that God is throwing you a lifeline and giving you the opportunity to experience freedom.

In John chapter 5, there's a story of a guy who lived with a dysfunction for thirty-eight years. That's a really long time to be stuck in one condition. Let's read the story:

> After this there was a feast of the Jews, and Jesus went
> up to Jerusalem. Now there is in Jerusalem by the

Sheep Gate a pool, which is called in Hebrew, Bethesda, having five porches. In these lay a great multitude of sick people, blind, lame, paralyzed, waiting for the moving of the water. For an angel went down at a certain time into the pool and stirred up the water; then whoever stepped in first, after the stirring of the water, was made well of whatever disease he had. Now a certain man was there who had an infirmity thirty-eight years. When Jesus saw him lying there, and knew that he already had been in that condition a long time, He said to him, "Do you want to be made well?" The sick man answered Him, "Sir, I have no man to put me into the pool when the water is stirred up; but while I am coming, another steps down before me." Jesus said to him, "Rise, take up your bed and walk." And immediately the man was made well, took up his bed, and walked. And that day was the Sabbath (John 5:1-9).

Using this miracle as a backdrop, I have identified four barriers that prevent healing. But before moving on, I have a little disclaimer. If terms like "pain, hurt, wound or dysfunction" seem vague, it's on purpose. I chose not to label specific issues because then it alienates others not affected by it. My hope is that through self-reflection, the Holy Spirit will pinpoint the specific need in your life that must be healed.

1. Disguises

When Jesus asked the lame man, "Do you want to be made well?" He started making excuses why he couldn't get any better. In fact, he avoided the question all together. Instead of saying, "Yes! Please heal me!" he completely changed the subject. He replied, "Sir, I have no man to put me into the pool when the water is stirred up." This was a diversion, perhaps a way to avoid the real issue.

When Adam sinned in the Garden of Eden, he sewed fig leaves together to disguise his guilt. Even today, we have a tendency to disguise our hurts or sins. That's why God asked Adam, "Where are you?" Not because God didn't know where he was, but the reality was that Adam needed to face his failures. He needed to recognize his own need for wholeness.

Sometimes it's easier to live in denial and cocoon yourself with false beliefs rather than wrestle with the reality of your situation. But keep this in mind; miracles are never born out of lies. God can untangle your problems, so long as you're willing to admit them.

Touching Where It Hurts

My son Makai is an active four-year-old who loves to play rough. Like a lot of boys his age, he scrapes, bruises or bangs something just about every day. I grew up in a house of all boys, so scrapes and bruises come with the territory.

When Makai hurts himself, his first reaction is to come crying to me. And the first thing I usually say to him is, "Show me where it hurts". The only way I can help him is if I know where he's hurting.

Here's the problem: he doesn't let me touch it. For some reason he's always afraid I'm going to hurt him more. In a way, I understand because sometimes contact creates a fear of re-injury. Plus, it just feels uncomfortable (like when removing a splinter).

Like this example, sometimes we cradle our hurts out of fear of being hurt again and also because we simply don't understand our heavenly Father's love.

God is saying, "Let me touch where it hurts." Or, like He said to the lame man, "Do you want to be made well?"

James 5:16 says, "Confess your faults one to another, and pray one for another, that ye may be healed. The effectual fervent prayer of a righteous man avails much." There's a connection between confessing your flaws or hurts and being healed. Notice it says *confess*, not *complain*. To confess is to reveal, which leads to healing. Complaining only festers the problem. Too often we complain about things and actually block our own victory.

When Jesus asked the lame man if he wanted to be made well, he started complaining about his situation, "Sir, I have no man to put me into the pool when the water is stirred up; but while I am coming, another steps down before me." It is so easy to miss God's blessing because we complain and don't confess. It's time to remove your disguise and expose your real need. The only way God can heal you is for you to be honest about what or who is hurting you.

2. Friends (a.k.a. "Frenemies")

The lame man at the pool of Bethesda suffered for 38 years. And every day, a friend or neighbor would carry him to the porch where he could lay and wait for the waters to stir. His illness had developed to the point where he could not transport himself. He was immobilized and that's what hurts can do; they cripple us and keep us from pursuing our God-given purpose.

This lame man became entirely dependent on others. His friends had become his nurses but ironically, they did not promote change in his life. Their good intentions only dug a deeper hole for him.

We could also label them "frenemies". A frenemy is a combination of a friend and an enemy. It's basically someone who pretends to be a friend but is actually an enemy or enabler. I'm not saying that this man's friends were outright malicious; maybe they had good intentions. But if you're stuck in an unhealthy situation, you have to be challenged and empowered, not simply enabled to do the same thing day after day.

You have to be careful who you associate with. Don't underestimate the power of relationships and how they influence your life, for the better or worse. There are people who will just listen and agree with you, but won't confront you. They censor their true opinions because they want to stay neutral. They don't want to cause friction or disappoint you. They would rather be well liked, then helpful.

Of all the people who carried the lame man, nobody asked him the question that Jesus asked him: "Do you want to be made well?" How do I know that nobody asked him? I don't know for sure, but he seemed puzzled by the question. It appears he had never been challenged before. Instead, all he got was pity and a free ride. Sometimes real friends have to intervene in order to help you.

3. Apathy

I've wondered why Jesus would ask the infirmed man the question, "Do you want to be made well?" Initially, the question seems a bit patronizing. This guy was obviously distressed and incapable of living a normal life. Something was clearly wrong with his situation. He was crippled by some unknown condition with no hope in sight.

From the outside in, you would assume this man wanted to be healed.

However, when you live with a particular issue for a long period of time, you begin to accept and accommodate it. Sooner or later, apathy settles in.

This disabled man had become comfortably uncomfortable. Even though he sat at a place of hope, he felt hopeless and indifferent. His problem had become his identity.

Maybe you're thinking, "Wait a minute, he went to the pool of Bethesda daily. Wasn't that good enough?" Not necessarily. Coming and waiting near the pool had become part of his daily routine. At some point, he simply stopped expecting anything to happen. Everyday, it was the same script.

Come.

Sit.

Wait.

Leave.

His life had become so mechanical, it seemed he forgot why he was there to begin with.

Jesus asked "Do you want to be made well?" because He knew that this man had lost his sense of urgency. He knew that his desire had regressed into the pit of religious rhetoric and mediocrity. Does that describe you in any way? Do you find yourself slipping into apathy even though your situation is getting worse? Have you stopped hoping?

If that's you in any way, shape or form, it's time to confront your apathy. It's time to fuel your faith.

How Bad Do You Want It?

Jesus asked this hurting man, "Do you want to be made well?" Apparently, Jesus wanted to ignite a fire within him.. Notice what Jesus didn't ask: "do you wish?" or "would you consider?" He said, "Do you **want**…"

In other words, how bad do you want it? Are you fed up enough with your condition to change it? Jesus is checking out your desire and faith today.

Jesus commanded the man, "Rise, pick up your bed, and walk". Essentially, pick up whatever is making you comfortable! Pick up the excuses, the fallback and the scapegoat that keeps you on the porch. Quit waiting around for people to feel sorry for you. Your issues are burning people out. Your neediness is pushing away the only good friends you've got left. Get fed up with your condition and fed up with your lifestyle. There's a miracle on the other side of your excuse.

4. Fear

Fear has many faces and ways of manifesting in our lives. I think it's important that we understand the difference between being *afraid* and having *fear*. Let's be honest. We all get afraid. If someone pointed a loaded gun at me, I wouldn't quote 2 Timothy 1:7. I would yell for help! That's not the *spirit of fear*. That's called being *afraid*. Let me explain:

- Being afraid is circumstantial. (The loaded gun is pointed at me.)

- Fear is spiritual or psychological. (No gun, no shooter. But I feel threatened.)

- Being afraid is for a moment. (The gun is pointing at me *right now*.)

- Fear is a lifestyle. (I don't want to see, hear or talk about guns.)

See the difference?

When Paul told Timothy, "For God has not given us a spirit of fear, but of power and of love and of a sound mind" (2 Timothy 1:7), he wasn't talking about being afraid, but about living in fear. The spirit of fear is the dominance of anxiety, where it alters your perception of reality and affects your spirit.

Being afraid flows from the outside in. Fear flows from the inside out. In other words, having fear is constantly seeing threats that don't always exist.

Here's how fear becomes a stronghold. After a while, you become convinced and accept false limitations. You end up living in a cocoon of worries, unable to possess God's promises and enjoy the victories we have in Christ. A thick crust of excuses and regrets form around your life and suffocate your dreams. Your cup of destiny is full of apologies instead of running over with joy and zeal for God.

Fear is cruel and relentless. Like the hurting man at the pool of Bethesda, it allows you a glimpse of healing and nothing more.

No More Excuses

Now that we understand fear a little more, we get a clearer picture of this hurting man. Jesus' question, "Do you want to be made well?" shifted his entire foundation.

When Jesus asked him the question, he offered a lousy excuse. Instead of responding with faith, he got defensive. Excuses are the offspring of fear. In other words, when you live in fear, the natural thing to do is make excuses as to why you cannot receive God's promises.

There isn't enough room on this page to list all the excuses and defenses people use. People in fear will say whatever they can to defend their indecision. They will invent reasons, conjure up stories and find loopholes to stay where they are. I suggest it's time to rebuke fear and stomp it down with the Word of God. His perfect love will cast out all fear (1 John 4:18).

The Mirror of Mercy

The crippled man in the story found himself at Bethesda, which is translated "house of mercy". However, fear turned his house of mercy into a house of horrors. Have you ever been inside a fun-house at the fair with those distorted mirrors? Those mirrors twist our view of anything we put in front of them. They can make you look tall or short, fat or thin. As kids we thought it was funny. But you might have a distorted mirror in your mind. That's nothing to joke about. If you're looking at a distorted mirror, you might think the images are real and permanent.

If your inner mirror is distorted, it will twist your view of yourself and everything else. If your mirror makes you look fat, you will look that way no matter how much weight you lose. If your mirror reflects a worthless person, no amount of love and acceptance will change how you feel about yourself. If your mirror only reflects your scars and wounds, you will always see yourself as a victim or damaged goods. A distorted image leads to a distorted lifestyle.

Satan is behind every distorted mirror—twisting, bending and stretching truths until they become lies. But Jesus Christ is the Healer who came to restore your image and heal your wounds. How is that possible? Jesus gives you His image, His righteousness and His power.

In Galatians 2:20, Paul declared, "I have been crucified with Christ; it is no longer I who live, but Christ lives in me; and the *life* which I now live in the flesh I live by faith in the Son of God, who loved me and gave Himself for me." The image you should see in the mirror is no longer that broken or distorted young adult. Rather, it is the merciful Savior Jesus Christ who covers your past and assures your future.

Stop trying to straighten out these distorted mirrors on your own. Positive thinking and self-help techniques are not going to solve the problem. These distorted mirrors in your mind must be replaced by the Gospel of Jesus Christ—the mirror of mercy. As you see yourself (healed and set free) in Jesus, your life will be transformed.

Maybe you have lost sight of God's mercy and His relentless love for you. Maybe you have wasted too much energy by catering to your wounds and blaming others for your problems. It's time to enter God's house, where mercy and grace abounds. Declare as David did: "But as for me, I will come into Your house in the multitude of Your mercy; In fear of You I will worship toward Your holy temple" (Psalm 5:7).

Shift Keys

1. Remove your mask – There is a tendency to hide our pain for fear of being judged or hurt again. Secrecy limits the power of Jesus Christ to transform your life. James 5:16 tells us, "Confess *your* trespasses to one another, and pray for one another, that you may be healed. The effective, fervent prayer of a righteous man avails much."

2. Confront your comfort – Have you accommodated your hurts so much that you have lost the desire for healing? The longer you cradle your issues, the easier it becomes to justify them. Jesus didn't die on the cross so that you could live a dysfunctional life. By His stripes we are healed. Perhaps it's time to believe God for greater things and ditch every crutch you're leaning on.

3. Walk in His mercy – The Bible tells us in Lamentations 3:22-24, "*Through* the LORD's mercies we are not consumed, because His compassions fail not. *They are* new every morning; Great *is* Your faithfulness. "The LORD *is* my portion," says my soul, "Therefore, I hope in Him!" God's mercy surrounds you and His faithfulness envelopes you. Keep your hope anchored on Jesus!

8 | Lovestruck

Friendship to Courtship

It may surprise you that the Bible doesn't mention the words "dating or courtship". However, that doesn't make the topic taboo. The Bible doesn't talk about wearing seatbelts in our cars, but most of us do. Why? We value the gift of life. The reality of dating, courtship and romance has to be treated in a similar manner where we use Biblical principles to guide our decisions and emotions in relationships.

I know us Christians are supposed to avoid the word "date" like the flu, because for many, it sounds too worldly. Well, I agree and disagree. One on hand, it's not a perfect term. But on the other hand, there aren't many other terms to choose from. The word "courting" isn't too bad, but for some, it sounds too old-fashioned. For others, it sounds too serious or too broad for the various stages of relationships. But since "courtship" is the safest term, I'll come back to that topic in a few pages.

Inevitably, other terms arise that don't really help either. For instance, *getting to know* or *just talking*. Technically, you are *getting to know* a lot of people—at school, at work and at church. Not a very useful term. And *just talking* sounds a little too junior high-ish.

So while the word "date" isn't perfect, I'm going to redeem it for the purpose of defining an area of life that often gets murky for young adults.

The Bible doesn't give us a Ten Commandments for dating or spouse-finding, but still, His Word is a lamp unto our feet and a light unto our path. We can use Biblical principles for relationships and custom-fit them for dating.

There are some core truths to help young adults pilot the turbulent skies of romance. I can't promise you a journey without bumps or dips of emotion, but I can assure you that by allowing truth to guide you, your relationships will be healthier and better off. My goal in writing this chapter is not to give you a quick solution or tell you when you'll meet the right person. Quite honestly, this subject deserves its own book. I simply want to smash some myths and provide some Biblical guidance for relationships.

Before I continue, let me remind you that the target audience of this book is young adults in their 20's to early 30's. If you're younger than that, I still encourage you to read and learn. But if you're in this age range, I hope you will give deeper thought and consideration to these words.

Singled Out By God

Perhaps you've heard the myth that finding the right one "completes you". It sounds romantic. But it's really not true, even if it's what Jerry Maguire (Tom Cruise) so famously said in the romantic comedy film *Jerry Maguire*. To make my case, let's go back—way back—all the way to the Garden of Eden.

It's been ingrained in us that marriage is the foundation of human society. Although I understand the premise of this theory, it's a bit flawed. The actual foundation of human society, as God imagined, was a *single* individual. When God scooped dirt into his hands and sculpted the first human—he was whole, complete and good. To believe that the first human, Adam, was incomplete would be an insult to his Creator.

I think many of us are guilty of viewing singleness through the lenses of tradition and social norms. As a result, many singles and non-singles tend to form views about singleness that are mostly negative and unbiblical. Maybe these views are not expressed openly, but it's certainly the undercurrent of conversation or the punch line of humor.

For example, some view singleness like it's a curse or sign

that something is "wrong with them". If you're over the age of 25 and don't have a boyfriend/girlfriend, are not engaged or married, people tend to judge you or assume that something about you makes you "undateable" or defective.

To say it plainly, being single carries a stigma in our society and it also bleeds into the Church—evident by some fairly anemic theories. So perhaps I can debunk two common misconceptions by identifying what singleness is "not".

1. Singleness is Not a Test

I have to admit that when I hear people rationalize singleness as a test or trial for Christian singles, it makes me a little crazy. Nowhere in Scripture is singleness considered a test of any sort. Sure, we can point to certain examples like Joseph and how he resisted temptation as a young single man, or how Samson caved in and laid his head on Delilah's lap.

But in those cases as with all the others, singleness was merely a reality and not the object of the lesson. By this rationale, nearly all of Joseph's life lessons would be irrelevant to married people since most of his trials took place before marriage. Also, by this rationale we would come to see childhood, marriage and widowhood as tests. Certainly we wouldn't tell a widowed woman that God is using her widowhood as a test. He wouldn't because we know it's just a stage of life or human experience.

Of course, God can test your faith *during* your single years, but Scripture doesn't suggest that He's using the state of singleness as the test itself.

The *singleness-is-a-test* camp would say something like, "as soon as you're satisfied with God alone, you'll find someone special". If I were a single person who had a strong relationship with Jesus Christ, I would be frustrated by that viewpoint. The truth is, a lot of singles are satisfied with God and still haven't met the right one yet. Now of course, if you keep loving and serving God, you will attract the right type of person.

Ruth is a good Biblical example. She followed God's call to Bethlehem and there she met Boaz. She married God first, so to speak. She made vows unto God, but that still isn't proof that being satisfied with God guarantees you a husband or wife. Ruth still had to meet Boaz at the threshing floor and interact socially with him. You'll never meet anyone just loving Jesus all day in your room and never going out to meet people.

2. Singleness is Not God's "Plan B"

Another false notion about singleness is that it's like a back-up plan in case marriage isn't in your immediate future. I've heard married couples talk about single young adults as if God needs to grant them extra grace—almost to suggest that being single isn't God's best.

If you really want to split hairs, marriage was more like

God's "Plan B" if one existed. Let's not forget, God created a singular man and said it was "good". He was a complete and intact human.

Adam enjoyed this period of life when it was just him and God. As a single man:

- He was responsible (protected the garden)
- He had a job (tended the garden)
- He was intelligent (named all the animals)
- He was close to God (walked with God in the cool of the day)

Furthermore, singleness is smiled upon in the New Testament. In 1 Corinthians 7:7-8, the Apostle Paul implies that singleness is a gift from God, just like marriage. In verses 32-35, he describes the challenges of being married and the freedom a single person has to serve the Lord without distractions. And in Matthew 22:30, Jesus explains that marriage is a temporary union which doesn't continue in heaven, thereby dismantling the notion that marriage is God's premium choice.

Just to be clear, I'm not saying that marriage is bad and singleness is better, or vice versa. The point I'm making is that it's not either/or, but both/and when it comes to marriage and singleness. I'm simply leveling the playing field and putting to rest the idea that marriage ranks higher or that God is just tolerating your singleness.

What I'm going to say next could be misinterpreted, but hopefully it just adds perspective. If marriage is Plan A and singleness is Plan B, then Jesus Himself lived a "Plan B" life because he was a single man his entire earthy life, all 33 years. That might just shatter the idea that God *wants* you to be married or that it's your destiny to be married. Here's the bottom line. Marriage is a choice.

To be clear, this isn't a denial of God's involvement in our decision-making or His ability to bring two people together. Neither is God playing cupid against your will nor putting you and your potential partner under a spell of love. God's typical approach is described in Psalm 37:4: "Delight yourself also in the Lord, and He shall give you the desires of your heart."

Heavenly delight is the catalyst of human desire. Notice that God doesn't tell us *what* our desires should be. He simply wants to be our highest pleasure, our addiction and source of fulfillment. He craves our craving and seeks our seeking. When we delight in God and marinate in His goodness, our desires become a reflection of His desires. In other words, God will give you the desires of your heart because more than likely…He inspired them.

This is true especially in relationships. God doesn't necessarily pick your mate, but rather He guides us with wisdom and values.

Let me shift gears and give you some practical help. Maybe you've been accused of being "too picky". This makes it seem like God is annoyed by your preferences and needs broader parameters to work with.

Really?

I doubt that God has ever been in a pinch or sweated out the fine details of life. Plus, how would your future spouse feel about themself if they knew you lowered the bar to marry him/her? Not exactly a compliment.

We don't usually say you're being "too picky" about anything else in life. You're never accused of being too picky when you're buying a car, choosing a school, buying a house or even a pair of shoes!

Pickiness isn't the problem. Assuming that one person can meet *all your needs* is the real problem.

As long as your expectations are realistic and not built on fantasy, I think single young adults should be picky about who they date, court and eventually marry. Just be willing to recognize your own flaws and dysfunctions before expecting perfection in someone else. That should keep you grounded and your pickiness balanced.

From Friendship to Courtship

Now that I've established the importance of singleness in God's eyes, this chapter couldn't be complete without a conversation about courtship. As stated earlier, I realize that the term sounds old-fashioned and is not used much in everyday language. But it may help to define a process in relationships that often gets scrambled with emotions and misread signals.

In his book, *Boy Meets Girl: Say Hello to Courtship*, author Joshua Harris identified three areas that we need to grow and guard for courtship to be successful (whether it comes to marriage or not). The three areas are: *friendship, fellowship, and romance.*[9] I concur with Harris and believe that you should observe these areas and how they develop in your life. Using Harris' terms, I'll add my own interpretation.

1. Friendship

The friendship stage in dating relationships (pre-courtship) is commonly skipped. I've seen this happen so many times.

Here's the scenario: After meeting each other or reconnecting, three weeks go by and the "friends" are already saying "I love you" and holding hands. Before you know it,

---

[9] Harris, Joshua (2009-10-05). Boy Meets Girl: Say Hello to Courtship (Kindle Locations 963-964). Random House, Inc.. Kindle Edition.

their relationship status gets updated on Facebook to "in a relationship", followed by weeks of Instagram pictures of the two lovebirds at Starbucks or Chili's. Then suddenly, his or her Facebook account goes dormant and status updates freeze in time. A week later his relationship status is changed back to "single".

Rewind this scenario and press play about three times over and now you have a picture of dating in the 21st century.

I admit that I trivialized the issue just a little. But to me it's painfully obvious that a couple like this never developed an actual friendship. Young adults who rush into relationships typically focus more on sparking romance, physical touch and want to quickly figure out if they're compatible. But genuine friendships take time to develop, through a course of conversations, appropriate group time together and learning about each other (including their families).

Young adults feel pressured into commitment and exclusivity. This behavior creates an unhealthy momentum where both sides are trying to meet each other's needs prematurely. In the process of doing so, they monopolize each other's lives and feel forced to validate their love with deeper acts of affection.

Rushed relationships typically thrive on physical attraction, therefore making it even more difficult to be clear about boundaries. And if you're in a state of depression or hurt, the other person will become your emotional drug addiction, your fix.

There is a better alternative to developing a solid relationship. It would be wise to build an authentic friendship without forcing yourselves into each other's lives or arms. You don't have to text each other every five or ten minutes. Let your conversations be meaningful, respectful and centered on something other than romance. Treat each other as you would any other friend.

Don't apologize for giving other people attention. If he or she gets jealous of your other friends, I've got two words for you: *red flag*. Either they are insecure or don't know how to have functional friendships. Either way, it's a sign that things need to slow down or stop all together.

2. Fellowship

In his book, Joshua Harris pointed out that: "Guarding the fruit of true Biblical fellowship means increasing your love and passion for God, not your emotional dependence on each other. Your goal is to point each other to Him. All the ideas shared for growing in fellowship have to be guarded from abuse. We should never use spiritual activities as a way to grab for more intimacy than is appropriate for our relationship."[10]

---

[10] Harris, Joshua (2009-10-05). Boy Meets Girl: Say Hello to Courtship (p. 81). Random House, Inc.. Kindle Edition.

Like any strong relationship, yours must be built on a solid spiritual foundation. Your spiritual passion, faith and convictions should not be an afterthought, but intentional. Maybe you get spiritual at the wrong time in relationships. Or you get *just enough* spiritual in order to keep your girlfriend from breaking up with you.

This happens either because one individual simply wants to impress the other or because he or she wants to use spirituality as a way of manipulating the other person. For instance, when someone says, "I prayed and God told me we belong together". This kind of phony spiritually can be avoided if the friendship is centered on Jesus Christ and involves the guidance of parents or mentors.

This is where discipleship can make a big difference. It's important that you and your boyfriend/girlfriend are being discipled separately by Godly mentors. Being accountable to your boyfriend/girlfriend doesn't count.

You should be accountable to someone else, preferably someone older and of the same sex. If possible, your parents should play an active role and their opinions should matter to you.

Whatever you do, don't rely solely on a mutual friend who may not always give you objective advice.

Missionary Dating

The area of spiritual fellowship will also guard you from *missionary dating*. That's a term to describe when a believer dates an unbeliever, hoping they will convert. We're taught in 2 Corinthians 6:14, "Do not be unequally yoked together with unbelievers. For what fellowship has righteousness with lawlessness? And what communion has light with darkness?"

Certain young adults are convinced that they can date an unbeliever and convert them to Christianity or the Apostolic Church.

That is a dilemma that surfaces when a Christian single is convinced that their future mate doesn't exist in the church, or they are simply love-struck by his charm or her beauty. Dating or courting someone of a different faith is a recipe for disaster. It may not feel like it right now, but sooner or later the issue of faith will cause problems in your relationship.

You have to make sure he or she is a genuine believer. Even if he is baptized and filled with the Holy Spirit, that doesn't automatically make him the best candidate.

Does he have a fruitful relationship with Jesus Christ? You simply cannot gamble your future on a whim that she will eventually convert or become a strong Christian.

Maybe you're trying to rationalize by pointing out all of his positive qualities. But if he ever becomes your husband, all of his good attributes will not compensate for the lack of spiritual oneness and leadership in the home.

Don't experiment with missionary dating. You could actually end up being the one who gets won over to the world. It's a high-risk relationship with very few success stories.

Okay, here's the final area to grow and guard for courtship to be successful.

3. Romance

Ideally, romance would develop *after* friendship and fellowship have already occurred. This way the relationship has the foundation which to build upon and the guardrails to protect against dangers. Romantic feelings are not evil. If submitted to God, romance can produce appropriate expressions of care and sincere love. Let's remember one thing: God created love. In fact, God *is* love. No one understands romance better than God. He literally wrote the book on it.

In Ephesians 5:25 it says, "Husbands, love your wives, just as Christ also loved the church and gave Himself for her." Jesus Christ is the ultimate picture of romance as seen through His epic love story of redemption. God instructs men to love their wives like He loves the Church. In other words, God is saying, "If you want to know what romance is, just watch the way I treat My Church—my bride".

Romance is expressed differently depending on your relationship level. Also, romance should look different between a married couple and a non-married couple. One clear distinction is physical affection and sexual intimacy. Sex is reserved for marriage and is sacred in that context (Ref. Gen. 2:24, Heb. 13:4). Sex, sensual activity or thoughts outside of marriage are forbidden (Ref. Matt. 5:28, 1 Cor. 6:18, 1 Cor. 7:1, 1 Thess. 4:3-4).

These aren't some outdated rules made up by old-school traditionalists. This is the Word of God. It can't be modernized or abused by a cheap brand of grace that says "it's okay to have sex with your boyfriend or girlfriend as long as you keep repenting and can feel God's presence on Sunday". Also, don't believe the lie that says "it's okay to have sex or do sexual favors as long as you two get married". Maybe my tone is becoming a little preachy, but I sense that a young unmarried adult will read this section and feel convicted by the Holy Spirit to stop having sex.

There could also be a deeper reason why your sexuality is destructive. If you're a young man, maybe your father, uncle or older brother told you that romance was purely about sexual encounters with women. Maybe that's your only definition of love. Be assured that God can set you free from that mindset.

If you're a young lady, maybe you were taught that women are sexual objects and must do whatever a man says. Maybe if you were abandoned, raped or molested you feel worthless and therefore sex is your attempt to prove your love and value.

Regardless of what twisted concept you have of romance and love, God wants to purify your soul and renew your mind for healthier relationships. It's not too late to break this destructive pattern. Through God's power and grace, you can develop relationships that are sexually pure and God-honoring.

Bad Romance

In the past five years I've traveled throughout the country speaking to young adults about dating and relationships. Not only have I been able to share what I know, but also have been learning about what this generation thinks about relationships and how the "game" is played. What I've learned is that many young adults already find themselves stuck in relationships and don't know what to do.

I always get that "I'm already in love" scenario presented to me. Those people who pull me aside for help are usually already involved with someone and unsure how to navigate their way through or out of the relationship. Rarely do people ask for advice *before* they enter a relationship.

It's hard to remember the last time a young man or lady approached me for advice before meeting someone. Usually, they're already seeing someone or just got dumped and are hurt.

Over the years, I have received tons of emails from young adults who are webbed in unhealthy relationships. Using real questions and answers, here are three signs of "bad romance". (To protect their privacy, the names presented are fictitious). I should also warn you that all of these questions are from young ladies, who are usually the ones asking for advice.

1. False Expectations

Question from Lauren:

"I currently have a boyfriend. We've been together for six months but have known each other for almost our whole lives. Before this weekend, things had been pretty bad and we almost broke up. In many areas of our lives we don't match, yet I've been holding on because I believed in change and thought that I could be that one person that could help him become a better version of himself.

As sad as it sounds, when I read the descriptions that you wrote of Mr. Wrong in your article, I felt like he was one of them. The reason why I said he fit that description is because when we came back from this weekend's activity, he came back with a different mindset. He told me he wants to change and he believes we can do great things for the Lord together. He wants to pray more together and is more receptive of my busy life. He also told me that he needs me in order to change, and that he doesn't have a male role model, therefore it's a lot harder for him to change alone.

These are things that I prayed about for a long time and longed to hear him say these things, but now I can't help to feel like it's too late. I can't help to feel like why should I put up with the 'under construction' process and at the same time, I feel like I should give him a chance to change.

I am really confused as to what I should do. Should I stay and wait for results or just break up and move on. I don't want to feel like I'm doing things just because I feel like the grass is greener on the other side but I am also scared of ending up with someone that will hurt my ministry.

Do you have any words of advice?" -*Lauren*

My Response to Lauren:

"Your question is a good one. A couple of things come to mind. First, your relationship with this young man seems unhealthy, especially since it's only been six months. Honestly, it sounds like he needs some growing up to do. Not to say he's not a nice guy or won't make a good husband one day. But he doesn't seem emotionally stable. He may need to resolve some of these personal issues before entering a serious relationship.

My opinion is that you need to give him and yourself some space. If it's truly meant to be, it will work out later.

You also need to be realistic, not just *idealistic*. Thinking that you could change him or that you could motivate him to change is not fair. Until he's motivated himself, only then will he change. That being said, you should give him space and time to see if he'll change on his own, or without being your boyfriend. His motivation needs to be rooted in God.

Lastly, what does this say about his state of mind or how he handles pressure? If he's relying on you, that's not a good sign. In marriage, the man should be the strong leader, the support for the family and wife. While I do empathize with his misfortunes in life, you should avoid being his therapist because that will create a pattern for future problems.

I hope this helps you make your decision. You must decide for yourself and use common sense. I know the Lord will guide you and speak to your heart. Just listen close." *-Jacob*

2. Bad Timing

Question from Jennifer:

"I've recently heard a conference you presented called, "When God Writes Your Love Story". I had a question about something you said. "If it's the right thing at the wrong time, it's the wrong thing". Can you go into further detail with that? I didn't quiet understand it.

I ended a relationship like 3 or 4 months ago. It's been hard; actually that whole relationship was chaos. I was definitely hurt a lot by this young man. I'm just a little confused as to why I went through all of this.

Ever since I was a little girl I've always prayed to God to send me the right guy because I didn't want to date a lot of guys. It's just something I've always asked for. But now that all this happened to me, I'm wondering, did God not answer my prayer? I don't know, just something I wanted to share with you. This guy hurt me a lot and I don't know why I can't seem to let it go." *-Jennifer*

My Response to Jennifer:

"I'm sorry that you were hurt so badly by this relationship. Breakups are never easy.

"The right thing at the wrong time is the wrong thing" is basically saying that if the right type of person comes at the wrong time in your life, it's not going to work. People have to be ready (i.e. mature, available, spiritual, etc.) for relationships. Timing plays a vital role in relationships.

Two types of love should be avoided: 1) Premature love – by this I mean love that rushes past friendship and into romance. 2) Immature love – by this I mean when two individuals simply haven't grown enough personally to be able to love someone and commit. It could be that your relationship with this young man suffered from both negative types (premature and immature). The solution is "time" and a lot of it. It sounds like you need to give yourself time to grow some more, spiritually and emotionally.

For your second question, "did God not answer my prayer?" This is not a question I think I can answer. I think you know the answer deep within. But consider this: why would God send you someone to purposefully hurt you? God isn't like that. God will not impose his will on us nor will he stand in our way from doing what we want. In other words, we all have our choice, our free will. Maybe this guy was more about what you wanted then what God wanted.

I'll finish with this advice. Don't worry or stress yourself by praying for God to send you someone. I'm not saying prayer isn't important in choosing the right person. It's important! What I'm saying is, trust in God by focusing purely on your relationship with Him and trust that He will send someone in the future. Prepare yourself. Grow in the Lord.

Consider this. God chose Adam and Eve for each other and neither one of them prayed for a mate. Adam went to sleep and woke up next to his dream wife. Enjoy your relationship with God, and when you're ready, and your future mate is ready, God will bring you two together." *-Jacob*

3. Not Letting Go

Question from Sandy:

"I have a question. I was talking to a guy where I thought

things were gonna work out. The problem is that he has a little girl. He was raised in church, but left, got married and got divorced.

I saw something very different in him that made me fall for him. We talked when we went out, and he told me he was being honest in that he was not ready for a relationship, and that he still talks to girls like from his past. That bugs me.

We both decided to be friends, but for girls it's never easy to leave a feeling you had for someone. So I asked him if he liked someone. He said he told me he wanted to be honest with me, about something else.

He told he was speaking to someone after he told me he wasn't ready for a relationship. He mentioned that it was not going to work out anyways. Knowing how I felt about him, he didn't really care. We stayed completely as friends, but when we go out with my friends he gives one girl attention that he never gave me.

Now my question is, is it wrong for me to assume something can be going on? And if it is true what am I assuming, what can I do to not to let it get to me and show him I can be a friend? I don't know what to do? Can you give me advice please?" -*Sandy*

My Response to Sandy:

"Thank you for contacting me. First, you need to ask

yourself if this is worth your time, effort and emotion. It doesn't seem smart to hold on to any hopes that he would fall for you too. Every day you spend thinking, trying, assuming or worrying about this, is a wasted day.

What I'm going to say next is going to be very hard to hear and swallow. I don't believe you should even continue a friendship with him. This relationship is not healthy and can become toxic to other important relationships in your life. This doesn't mean that you have to hate him now, or that you don't treat him politely. But he should become an acquaintance, not a close friend. It's not healthy for two people with love interests to try to remain friends because someone always gets hurt.

Being a friend to him is not helping you—it's hurting you. So, think about how you can "move on" from this and let go."
-Jacob

Learn Before You Love

In conclusion, I believe in something called "smart love", where adults love wisely and reject twisted definitions of romance. I urge you to love not only with your heart, but with your head. Be intelligent about your relationships. Think about the life you might live, good or bad, if you married this person. Don't allow temporary emotions decide your future. If you're patient, you will meet the right person at the right time.

Shift Keys

1. Enjoy singleness – Based on what you've learned about singleness, you should enjoy it instead of wasting time "wishing" you had somebody. Devote yourself to causes you care about and take full advantage of the freedom you have to learn, travel and create.

2. Let love simmer, not boil – When meeting someone special, don't feel pressured to rush into things. If he or she lights a fire in your heart, let it simmer through friendship instead of boiling with premature romance. Don't adjust the temperature (commitment level) until the time is right and you are clear about your intentions.

3. Keep yourself grounded in reality – Sometimes romance and emotions can cloud reality. Make sure you're not "in love with the idea of being in love". Don't sugarcoat a truth about someone to gain the approval of your family and friends. Instead of responding to criticism with, "you don't know him like I know him", take a step back and be sure you really know that person.

Part 3: Forward Shifts

9 | Power Trips

Gather to Scatter

As Oneness Apostolics, we preach and experience the baptism of the Holy Spirit, in accordance with Acts 2:38. Beyond the doctrinal implications, we enjoy the full expression and demonstration of the Holy Spirit. However, I want us to consider Jesus' promise in Acts 1:8, an often quoted and beloved Scripture of Pentecostals. The issue is that we tend to celebrate only half of this Scripture:

"But you shall receive power when the Holy Spirit has come upon you…"

Insert: praise, handclaps, tongues and maybe an aisle runner.

Okay, maybe a slight exaggeration.

I mean no offense. I'm proud to be an Apostolic. I was born and raised in this. I received the gift of the Holy Spirit at the age of 12 and it's a memory that I hold dear to my heart. I haven't stopped speaking in tongues ever since. I'm not ashamed of my Apostolic roots. It's who I am!

There's no problem with celebrating and enjoying what that Scripture declares. But I humbly suggest we also celebrate the second half of the verse.

"…and you shall be witnesses to Me in Jerusalem, and in all Judea and Samaria, and to the end of the earth."

Jesus gave us the Holy Spirit to go on "power trips". When most of us hear the words "power trip", we think of someone whose power or authority has gone to their heads and now they act arrogant. I'm referring to a different kind of power trip, the kind where by the power of the Holy Spirit we become witnesses of Jesus Christ and transport the Gospel to the ends of the earth.

I believe we need more young adults who are willing to go on power trips (based on my new definition), and step outside of their comfort zones and subcultures and reach the world around them. Jesus said to witness in Jerusalem, all of Judea and Samaria, and to the end of the earth. What does that mean, exactly? Here's a quick breakdown:

Jesus is saying, "You will be my witnesses, in your Jerusalem (your family or friends,) your Judea and Samaria (your community) and the end of the earth (all nationalities)."

Let's not become satisfied with recycling Pentecost, where

we just absorb but never release. There are still many millions who haven't heard the Oneness Gospel. It's time to plan your next power trip and complete Acts 1:8 in your life.

Our power trips could also be viewed as "fishing trips". Like Jesus' disciples, we are called to be "fishers of men" (Ref. Matthew 4:19). I'm not a great fisherman or outdoorsman, but I do know that there's more than one way to catch a fish. Most fishermen carry a tackle box filled with different types of lures, baits and hooks to catch whatever type of fish they want.

You have been empowered to reach the unreached with the Gospel, to fish for people. Signs and wonders should follow you as you extend yourself to those who are hurting, searching and bound in sin. You carry the hope of the world and His name is Jesus Christ.

Now, let's get practical.

Embarking on the subject of evangelism isn't as easy as it sounds. Let's be real. One reason is that a high percentage of us don't share our faith on a regular basis. Therefore, some guilt is attached to evangelism because it's one of those things we know we're *supposed to do*, but don't do enough. The sooner we acknowledge that reality, the sooner we can have a purposeful conversation about how to reach our generation.

Over the years I've seen just about every tactic, from door-knocking to street marching, concerts to healing crusades, tracts to tent revivals, live dramas to movie nights, marketing campaigns to community services. If someone is saved because of any of these efforts, I praise God.

However, I am optimistic about the resurgence of small groups and modeling ourselves after the early church (Ref. Acts 5:42). Admittedly I'm a student, not an expert on the subject of small groups. If your church is transitioning to a "small groups" church, I encourage you to immerse yourself in that culture and learn how to open your own small group. In my church, we call them "Life Groups" and I currently lead one that meets once a week. It's an amazing journey.

The purpose of this chapter is to engage you to think about evangelism as a whole and what exactly we are called to do. As a young adult, you are given the same commission as the entire Church body. Evangelism is not something you graduate into after high school or college, or after getting married. Evangelism is not a formal program or public ministry. It's not something you necessarily *do*, but more of something you *are*.

The Dechurched Generation

As I write this book, there are volumes of other books being written on how to reach our postmodern, post-Christian generation. About every other week I come across a new and hip book by either a mega-church pastor or theorist who hopes to recharge and clarify the Church's mission. The current mantra of outreach is to *make disciples*, which is an honest attempt to recapture the New Testament model of evangelism. What "making disciples" actually means varies from one book to the next.

Perhaps this represents a revolt of the last 20 years of seeker-sensitive, wide-but-shallow growth the Evangelical Church experienced. Of course, the Oneness Pentecostal Church can't easily be lumped together with other mainline faiths. We've had our own unique history and growing pains over the years, but there is still something to learn here because the unreached don't usually make a distinction between Baptist, Protestant or Pentecostal. All they see is "Christian".

An observation of our culture reveals that while some mega-churches are reaching epic numbers, it's not the entire story. According to a 2009 *American Religious Identification Survey*, the number of Americans who claim no religious affiliation has nearly doubled since 1990, surging from 8 to 15 percent[11].

Granted this survey is now four-years-old, it's still reflective of our culture and how many unsaved people are truly *dechurched*, not necessarily *unchurched*. I know we like the term unchurched when describing lost people, but the reality is, no

---

[11] Barry A. Kosmin and Ariela Keysar (2009). "American Religious Identification Survey (ARIS) 2008" (PDF). Hartford, Connecticut, USA: Trinity College. Retrieved 2013-14-03.

other nation on the planet has been more "churched" than America. And now studies show a rising number of dechurched people.

As a young adult in your twenties or thirties, it's time to think more analytically about the church, this generation and our mission. You must expand your realm of thinking and experience the spiritual tension or the burden that oftentimes only pastors feel. If we're going to expand the Kingdom of God, let's spy out the land and understand what we're facing.

What this survey means is that these once-churched people had an experience that fizzled or a journey that ended with disappointment. In reality, people join evangelical churches for all sorts of reasons, sometimes because of their children's program, softball league, singles ministry, coffee house, or because they were loved in a time of need. But then they realized that after the ambiance wore off, the coffee got cold, or the compassion became superficial, nothing deeper was happening.

They got *churched*, but not *converted*; they were *touched*, but not *transformed*.

The reality is that many of your unsaved peers, friends, classmates and co-workers have encountered organized religion to some degree and it shaped the way they view Christians.

Many people have unfortunately been exposed to twisted forms of Christianity, either on television (slick preachers promising miracles for money), the Internet, angry bible-thumpers or the relentless protestors outside the courthouses, clinics and late-night club scenes. All of this happens without them ever stepping into a Church building or small group. Couple this reality with what Paul says, "For the message of the cross is foolishness to those who are perishing, but to us who are being saved it is the power of God" (1 Cor. 1:18).

So, where does this leave us? How do we reach the unreached and the dechurched in our society?

All Things to All Men

There is a common verse in the Bible that's almost always taken out of context. I'm referring to 1 Corinthians 9:22 where Paul shares his secret to evangelism: "...I have become all things to all men, that I might by all means save some." Is the apostle Paul advocating that Christians should become chameleons in our culture, embracing the lifestyle of sinners in order to reach them?

Not on your life.

A lot of Christians misinterpret this passage as a case to lowering our standards or compromising for the greater good of saving the lost. Based on that error, some are convinced that in order to win the world, we have to imitate it. However, Paul is not endorsing the maxim: "When in Rome, do as the Romans do". His whole point is that rather than being self-righteous or standoffish because of his status as an apostle, he intentionally builds bridges and creates inroads into communities where the Gospel isn't being preached.

There's not a shred of Biblical evidence to support the notion that the Church must become people-pleasers or become *like* the world in order to *win* the world. We've been called out of darkness into His marvelous light. Our light is the contrast that this world needs to see and that cannot be achieved if we dim our lights by embracing the lifestyle of the world.

The apostle Paul urges us to engage, not embrace. If we engage the world, love sinners and create inroads into their lives, we'll be able to share the Gospel message. Paul didn't cater to his listeners; he found ways to relate to them so that the good news could be received.

Over the past several years, I've had experiences where I learned to become "all things to all men" in order to save someone. Last year I encountered a young man who arrived at our church in East Palo Alto. I'll call him "Devon" to honor his privacy. His mother had been attending our Sunday service for a couple of months. One day I remember her asking for prayers for her son, because he was trying to move out of a rough area in New Orleans and start a new life.

I had already decided that I would share the Gospel with him, befriend him and help steer him in the right direction. But honestly, I didn't know what to expect. A few weeks and a long bus ride later he arrived. Then a couple of days after arriving he attended my Life Group with his mom. That's where I met Devon and that's when I realized that reaching him wasn't going to be easy.

We practically had nothing in common.

First of all, I'm 13 years older (all references to the 80's were officially out). He's Black. I'm Hispanic. He came from rough neighborhoods in New Orleans, Louisiana. I lived in a quiet, safe neighborhood in San Jose, California. He has tattoos; I don't. He came from a dysfunctional family, I didn't (that doesn't mean my family is perfect). He loves to work out at the gym; I don't (but should). He can rap; I can't (and won't even try).

We both love sports, especially football.

So, guess how I started conversations or rebooted them when things got quiet?

Here's a hint. I didn't talk about Jesus. *Not initially*.

We talked football.

I used football as an inroad to Devon's world. It was subtle. But those little bridges eventually became highways as I was able to share the Gospel and baptize him in Jesus' Name!

I didn't change who I was or my convictions. I didn't start

sagging my pants or listening to rap music in order to identify with him. I simply maximized what we had in common and minimized what we didn't. This is what personal evangelism is about. Eventually, through prayer, something deeper occurs as the Holy Spirit works in and through you. Then discipleship starts to happen.

Outreach that Reaches Out

In John chapter 4, Jesus met a Samaritan woman at a well. If you're familiar with the story, you'll remember that Jesus confronted her lifestyle in prophetic fashion. He simply "read her mail". Once the intimate details of her life were revealed, she replied, "Sir, I perceive that You are a prophet" (John 4:19). This one conversion sparked a revival as the Samaritan returned home and testified that "He told me all that I ever did" (John 4:39). Because of one transformed life, many came to Christ and professed Him the Savior of the world.

But let's rewind the story.

Before the multitudes were saved. Before Jesus revealed His identity and said, "I who speak to you am *He*" (John 4:26). Before her sinful relationship was exposed. Before they discussed issues like worship and doctrine. (Yeah, a lot happens in this scene). Before any of that, how did they arrive to this point?

It all started when Jesus crossed over social barriers and entered Samaria. John 4:4 says, "He needed to go through Samaria". The words "needed to go" imply something urgent and crucial. This trip wasn't a detour. Jesus had every intention of going through Samaria and meeting this woman. In doing so He broke traditions and conventional wisdom by stepping foot into a region that was not only looked down upon, but avoided. Jesus crossed over the following barriers:

1. **Religious barrier** – As evident in their conversation, Jews and Samaritans had different views on God and religious customs. Among other things, there was an ongoing dispute about where the epicenter of worship should be—on a mountain or in the temple.

2. **Racial barrier** – Samaritans were technically a mixed race (half Jew, half Gentile) and therefore shunned by pure Jews. They were treated with deep prejudice and viewed as second-class citizens.

3. **Gender barrier** – When the disciples saw Jesus talking with the Samaritan woman, they were a little tense and confused (Ref. John 4:27). This was because a Jewish man would never normally speak with a woman alone. As a rabbi, this would have ended his career.

I'm often amused at believers who say they want to reach

the lost but don't adjust their life patterns to make conversation and relationships possible. I'm equally amused by people who live as if evangelism happens by accident, without effort or without taking intentional steps. If your social circle is made up mostly of Christians, it's not hard to see why it's difficult to reach the lost. Your life is populated with mostly "found" people.

The Samaritan woman could be seen as the poster-child for both the unchurched *and* dechurched, depending on the lenses you view her with. She was obviously living in sin and far from God (unchurched). But she also had a religious background and strong opinions to go along with it (dechurched). Therefore, this encounter wasn't easy and clean – which is what most of us want. Here are two words to describe this scenario: inconvenient and risky.

But Jesus doesn't allow any of these things to interfere with His mission. He knew that to do "outreach", you actually have to "reach out". As Apostolic believers, we cannot allow ourselves to be sucked into the bubble of our own subculture. We cannot allow church involvement (choir practices, meetings, Sunday services, concerts and preaching conferences) to substitute for authentic outreach and personal evangelism. We must refuse religious additives that quench our thirst for revival and deafens our ears to the sound of hurting communities.

When was the last time you found yourself engaged in a messy, inconvenient or risky attempt to save someone?

Going back to my friend Devon.

It got messy, inconvenient and risky at times. Some days I was a taxi, giving him rides to and from Life Group and other places. Other days I was a counselor, in-person or on the phone helping him cope with his emotions. And at times I was a job hunter, helping him search and fill out applications. Not every story of evangelism will look like this, but there must be a burden and willingness to engage the lives of people who are far from God.

What barriers exist between you and the unreached people around you?

More importantly, how do you cross over in a personal, but nonintrusive way?

To answer that, let's look again at Jesus and how He masterfully conversed with the Samaritan.

Making the Connection

I believe that one conversation has the power to open doors for the Gospel. Maybe it sounds crazy. But I think it's time to retrain our minds and discover how contagious we can be. If our lives are truly to be lived for the purpose of spreading and demonstrating the Gospel, we then have to recognize opportunities when they come. We cannot afford to simply "wait" for something to happen or a special sign that gives us permission to act. Jesus already commissioned us to "go and make disciples of all nations" (Matthew 28:19).

I think it would be helpful to deflate some common fears that we have about witnessing and sharing our faith. Here are a few that I've experienced:

- **Fear of rejection** – The honest truth is that many of us don't witness because we fear being rejected. But remember, if someone rejects the Gospel, they are declining the offer and not always you as a person. Also, just because they're not interested right now doesn't mean they won't be later. But I must warn you that evangelism is not rejection-proof. You can and will be rejected and "unfriended" at some point…if you're actually sharing your faith. Jesus was rejected too. And it hurts. That's just the reality.

- **Fear of not knowing what to say** – Some are scared that when they talk, they'll get tongue-tied or say the wrong thing. Remember, you don't need be to perfect or rehearsed—just be yourself. You don't have to explain the whole Bible from Genesis to Revelation. But do read the Word of God and hide it in your heart because you should have an answer to why you believe what you do. Responding with "I don't know, I just do" is unacceptable.

- **Fear of embarrassment** – Some fear that they will be embarrassed or make the other person feel awkward. Remember, it's all in your approach. Be clever about when and where you bring up the subject of Jesus, but also realistic. People get a little tense when you bring up religion or even Jesus. So, expect some degree of awkwardness and don't let it stop you. Know that the Holy Spirit will empower you to be His witness.

Bringing people to Jesus requires a personal connection. After all, most times we are the first impression people have of Jesus Christ or Christianity. Let's continue looking at Jesus' encounter with the Samaritan woman. I want to help you discover three keys to making an evangelistic connection.

1. Move slow

Jesus' conversation with the Samaritan woman started with a question: "Will you give me a drink?" (John 4:7). Sometimes there's a tendency to rush or force the issue upon people. For instance, if you try to turn every conversation into a Bible study, people might get turned off. Take your time. Invest into their interests before you expect them to invest into yours. Jesus asked a basic question that every human being can relate to.

Be careful not to take over the conversation. People want to be heard. Give them your listening ear.

2. Keep it simple

I also caution you about using "Christianese" or lingo that wouldn't make sense to an unchurched person. Telling someone how *powerful your worship services are* won't mean much of anything.

Take initiative and but keep things simple. Build relationships with people and look for practical ways of introducing Jesus Christ or spiritual topics. Jesus kept his approach simple by focusing on things that the Samaritan woman understood. In addition, He didn't start by talking about spiritual things. Maybe your evangelistic connection will start with treating someone to dinner, a game of basketball or a drink at Starbucks.

3. Be sensitive to their needs

Jesus told the Samaritan woman, "If you knew the gift of God and who it is that asks you for a drink, you would have asked him and he would have given you living water" (John 4:10). Jesus immediately recognized a spiritual thirst in her heart—without her even admitting it. Jesus had great interpersonal skills. He could read body language, moods, and personalities with accuracy. And it wasn't just because He was God and had unlimited knowledge. As a compassionate human, Jesus paid attention, listened and watched carefully.

4. Seek to understand

Not only did Jesus leverage his relational skills, but he focused first on her needs, not His. It wasn't until later that He mentioned His search for true worshippers. Creating a connection with someone happens when we think outside of our bubble of wants and needs. It happens when we refuse to live self-centered and make ourselves approachable. An old Chinese proverb says, "Seek to understand, before seeking to be understood." That makes a lot of sense.

I encourage you; don't wait for the church's annual revival, for Christmas or the Easter program, or a summer concert to share God's love. Build bridges with people and win their friendships. Let them see you live like a Christian. Then strategically pray for their salvation or whatever needs they have. Then invite them to a friendly gathering, a small group or Sunday service. Some fish are ready to jump into the boat and come to church. Some need to be lured over time.

Our greatest commission is to save a lost and dying world

(Matthew 28:19). However, many Christians cringe when they hear the word "evangelism". Likely because older evangelism tactics were too confrontational or required a gregarious personality. But if you truly understand that it's all about a personal connection, you'll find that it's the most natural thing you can do. That doesn't mean it won't require some effort or practice, but you will definitely find your personal role both exciting and rewarding.

Shift Keys

1. **Burst your bubble** – examine yourself and ask if you're living in a Christian bubble where most if not all your friends are Christians. Do you speak too much Christianese? Do you clam up around non-believers? Maybe it's time to burst your bubble and engage your community in daring ways. It's difficult to save the lost if you don't know or interact with lost people

2. **Build a bridge** – find something you have in common with an unsaved friend and leverage that for evangelism. It can be almost anything, as long as it doesn't compromise your beliefs or convictions. The point is to build a bridge with people so the Gospel can be carried over. It's practically cliché now, but I'll say it anyways: people usually want to *belong* before they *believe*.

3. **Bombard heaven (and hell)** – prayer is the ultimate weapon in spiritual warfare. Reaching people for Christ cannot be accomplished without prayer and fasting. Therefore, bombard heaven (and hell) with fervent prayer so that the chains of sin and bondage may be broken over that person's life. Go on a power trip!

10 | Beautiful Mess

Strength to Weakness

The summer of 1992 was epic. It was the year that the USA basketball team (a.k.a. "Dream Team") reclaimed gold in the Summer Olympics. That summer, I wore my Dream Team t-shirt until the caricatures and lettering faded out. 1992 was also the year that two strong earthquakes rocked California. My wife Cherie, who grew up in Southern California, still remembers that day and recalls how afraid she was.

But for me personally, 1992 was a year of destiny, the year when God called me. Of course, I didn't know it at the time. I was only 12-years-old. But as Jesus proved, 12-years-old is old enough to *be about my Father's business.*

It all began when I decided to surrender my life to Jesus Christ and was baptized on June 28, 1992. I'll never forget that day. I had the privilege of being baptized by my dad, who was also my pastor. In fact, this was during his first year of pastoring.

My dad and I stepped into the chilly waters of the baptismal tank and waited for the music to die down. My toes practically went numb. I knew how to hold my nose and when to gracefully fall back. As a preacher's kid, I had already seen many people get baptized. Plus, I had tons of baptizing experience in our swimming pool. Me and some other church kids would play in the pool and pretend to have baptisms. I must have baptized one of my friends a hundred times that summer.

Then the song leader held the microphone up to my dad. He prayed a blessing over me and then he baptized me in Jesus Name. When I came up out of the water, my dad pulled me in for a tight hug. There we were standing, soaked and hugging each other. I'm holding back tears just thinking about it. I can still feel his wet arms wrapped around me and him whispering in my ear, "Mijo, I'm here for you. We're going to help you." All I could do was weep and thank God.

Later that summer, I was filled with the precious gift of the Holy Spirit with the evidence of speaking with other tongues. I'll never forget the fire I felt inside. My body could barely contain the amount of love and power swirling around in my heart. My hands were lifted and tears cascaded down my cheeks. I thought to myself, *if this is God's presence...I want more.*

1992 was also the year God called me to preach.

Tape Sessions

I come from a long line of preachers and pastors. If people wonder why the sons of preachers often become preachers themselves, it's really not that complicated. If a boy grows up watching his dad, in many cases he decides to follow in his footsteps. Beyond that natural tendency, it is God who calls us, not ourselves.

My dad, Joseph V. Rodriguez, Jr., happens to be an Apostolic preacher. In 1992, he walked away from a lucrative career at IBM to become a full-time pastor. I still remember the day when he told us he was taking an early retirement from work to focus on the church.

Before my dad, my grandpa Joseph G. Rodriguez, Sr., was a dynamic preacher and church planter. Also, my grandpa Albert Salcido, my mom's dad, was an Apostolic minister, a gifted Bible college instructor and Spanish linguist.

As a kid, people always pegged me to be a preacher because my dad was and his dad was. Of course, not all preachers' sons are called to preach. But you know what? The label didn't bother me because at some point I realized that there was nothing else in the world I wanted to do more than preach the Gospel. So when God began to call me, I did what I thought I was supposed to do: I preached.

Tucked away in my dad's office are two audiocassette tapes. If you don't know what a cassette tape is, Google it. Anyhow, these two tapes are recordings of me preaching. In case you're imagining me preaching to a group of people inside a church, let me clarify. These recordings are of me preaching to myself in my bedroom. I had a small tape recorder and would actually record myself talking and preaching for hours.

Trust me; this isn't normal 12-year-old kid behavior. If you saw me then, you might have raised your eyebrows and thought, "What's up with this weird kid?"

But looking back, I realize that I did something I didn't know I was doing, something that we often fail to do.

I took my call literally.

The Lord spoke to me and said, "You're called to preach", and suddenly that's all I needed to get started. No one invited me to preach. No one saw me. No one was even listening! But there I was, *preaching* – messing up words, taking Scriptures out of context and rambling from one thought to the next. When I listen back, I can't even follow myself! That's how much I didn't make sense.

However, in another way, it made total sense. Maybe not what I said, but just that I *said something*. When I heard and recognized God calling me, my response was like young Samuel's, "Speak, for your servant is listening".

I wanted to share a little bit of my background because I think we take ourselves too seriously sometimes. We act like dynamic preachers were shuttled here from heaven and walk on clouds. We let ourselves believe that someone who's gifted is immune to weakness. How easily we forget just how normal, how human and how messy we all are.

Excellence vs. Perfectionism

We need excellence, but not perfectionism. Sometimes I wonder if we are creating a culture in the Church that professionalizes ministry to the point that no one is willing to embarrass themselves, attempt something bold or just plain act upon what God is calling them to do. I'm not advocating poor planning and bad organization. I'm just wondering if we're managing out the Holy Spirit and becoming too polished.

Ponder Acts 4:13 with me: "Now when they saw the boldness of Peter and John, and perceived that they were uneducated and untrained men, they marveled. And they realized that they had been with Jesus."

Now if you're an intellectual, professional or educated person, don't be nervous. I believe we need to excel in knowledge and build a better future for our families and churches. Ignorance is not a virtue. Neither is it a sign that one is more spiritual. I sincerely believe the Church, young adults in particular, should pursue higher education, advanced careers and ministerial excellence.

Personally, I am passionate about the Kingdom expanding into the marketplace and lecture halls. I myself am a career professional and work for a large corporation in the Silicon Valley. I interact with intelligent and educated business partners everyday. I disclose that not to boast, but to assure you that I'm not suggesting we dumb down our approach or view higher learning and career advancement in a negative light. We desperately need Apostolic voices in those arenas.

The key to Acts 4:13 are the words "uneducated" and "untrained". The Greek word for "uneducated" literally means "unlettered," suggesting the apostles were viewed as inexpert in terms of the rabbinical institution of the day. The Greek word for "untrained" denotes that these apostles didn't hold official positions or titles. In the eyes of the elite, they were just civilians.

What marveled the elites wasn't that these men were so unintelligent (because they weren't), but that despite formal training, they were amazingly bright and knowledgeable. Make no mistake about it, spending three-and-a-half years with Jesus Christ not only qualified them, but enriched their understanding far beyond any man-made institution. The religious leaders acknowledged this: "And they realized that they had been with Jesus."

Jesus was more than credible. Time and time again He schooled the Pharisees in the Mosaic Law and Old Testament Scriptures. After all, Jesus is *the Word* made flesh (See John 1:14).

In addition, these apostles were accomplished in their secular careers. One example is Peter. He wasn't some babbling drunk sailor. Peter was a successful business owner, a skilled fisherman who understood mathematics and oceanography. He was sharp.

However, when it came to ministry and preaching the Gospel, they relied on something other than human intellect. There was unmistakable evidence of their authority. Acts 4:14 says, "And seeing the man who had been healed standing with them, they could say nothing against it." The critics couldn't argue with a miracle. The lame man who used to beg in front of the temple gate was now healed and standing on his own two feet (See Acts 3:1-9).

Let's go back to Peter. Because even though he wasn't a *babbling* sailor, he was at times…a *cussing* sailor.

He also sliced a guy's ear off.

And he also denied Jesus on three separate occasions.

Ministry is messy because people are messy. And just like Jesus had to reattach a man's ear to fix Peter's mistake, we have no idea how often God has to clean up our messes and touch people in spite of our efforts to "help" Him.

God didn't call us to be perfect. Yet somewhere along the line, we bought into the notion that being Christian meant being perfect. We obsess about things that God doesn't. We live and do ministry as if God's grace were nonexistent and He's totally relying on us to do the job right. We feel that if we don't "hit a homerun" that we somehow failed God. We act like if every time we minister, a panel of judges is scoring us and can decide our fate. We tend to compare ourselves with others we admire and feel inferior or defective because maybe we didn't get the same results.

We forget that we are human.

Perhaps we don't realize that the main point of ministry isn't chiefly about us managing God's mission, but enjoying *the God* of the mission. Isn't it true that God needs nothing and no one to accomplish what He wants (i.e. Creation)? If that's true, then why does He call us and use us? Why would a perfect God dwell in imperfect people for such a critical mission?

Beautiful Mess

Every year at Christmas time, my family has the tradition of putting puzzles together. My mom's dining room table transforms into a workstation where hundreds of puzzle pieces get scattered. We always arrange the pieces into piles by color and then assemble the borders of the puzzle to create a frame.

From there we start building towards the center until it's complete. It can take a few days before it's done.

I was working on a puzzle a couple of holidays ago when my son, Makai, who was 3-years-old at the time, ran up to the table. With his cute high-pitched voice, he said, "Can I help you daddy?"

"Sure you can," I said.

Then he climbed up on the chair next to me and started grabbing pieces from the pile. From the corner of my eye I could see him trying to figure out where to put the pieces. He would look up at me and try to mimic my movements. But really, he had no clue how to match the tiny pieces and lock them into place.

He was actually making it worse, *not* helping me. He kept trying to force pieces into the wrong spaces. He kept messing with the edges of the puzzle and shifted a few pieces out of place. Honestly, I got a little bothered once he started messing things up. After all, I was the one who worked on it and got it looking nice. Now my son was ruining it!

But then something happened.

He looked up at me with his rosy cheeks and big brown eyes and said, "I'm helping you daddy, huh?"

My heart sank.

Instead of enjoying this moment with my son, I was worried about him messing up the puzzle. In that moment I realized that the point of the puzzle wasn't just to finish it or perfect it, but rather to savor the time with my son. The puzzle was messed up, but it was a beautiful mess.

I don't want to downplay the importance of excellence in ministry and serving. I don't want to cheapen our mission to reach the world and love people. Other chapters in this book target those matters directly. However, there is an element to ministry that is similar my Christmas puzzle.

In reality, we are like my 3-year-old son. God doesn't technically need us to accomplish His purpose. God can raise up another generation at another time. He can do more with His pinkie finger then all the denominations and churches of the world combined.

What He wants more than anything is our relationship, our hearts. Ministry is an expression of your relationship with God. Jesus said, "You shall love the Lord your God with all your heart, with all your soul, with all your strength, and with all your mind,' and 'your neighbor as yourself" (Luke 10:27). Loving others is the overflow of loving God.

Called to the Caller

God is sufficient and self-adequate. God doesn't *need* our help; rather He *invites* our help. He has chosen us to combine our utter weakness with His supreme power to reach the world.

God has chosen to use human instruments (with all of our flaws) in conjunction with His Spirit to advance the Kingdom. What an incredible privilege we have to partner with Jesus' mission.

In 1 Corinthians 3:9, the apostle Paul revealed, "For we are God's fellow workers; you are God's field, *you are* God's building." The first part of this verse is usually understood to mean that we are co-working *with* God in ministry. But if you read the entire passage (Ref. 1 Cor. 3:1-17), Paul was actually trying to defuse sectarianism between him and Apollos.

Paul's point was that they were partners, united in fellow labor for Christ under the same authority.

Let's dispel the notion that we are somehow co-anything with God or micro gods, and that He *needs* our talent to accomplish things. If you're a trumpet player, your trumpet isn't playing music – you are. Your trumpet is only making sounds that you command it to make – through your embouchure, breathing and hand movements. Without the musician, the trumpet makes no sound and is useless. As finely crafted as it is, it would just be a piece of shiny scrap metal.

Ministry is not a company merger with God, where two entities join forces and equally bring something to the table. We are not God's co-pilot, apt to take over when He needs a break. Neither are we God's Vice-President, second in charge and able to run things when He's out. God calls us to serve and expand

His Kingdom as an outflow of our relationship with Him.

I think John 15:5 sums it all up. Jesus said, "I am the vine, you are the branches; he who abides in Me and I in him, he bears much fruit, for apart from Me you can do nothing". The fruit we bear, the success in ministry, are the results of Jesus' labor and our obedience. Without abiding in Jesus through a close relationship, we can't do anything.

My goal in this segment is not to make you feel worthless, but quite the contrary. When we see ministry from Jesus' eyes, we realize that He involves us primarily because He loves us. Whatever we do as a Church should be done out of love for God and love for people.

Like my son at the puzzle table, we in our human efforts and flaws actually hinder the mission at times. Or like Peter who cut a man's ear off, we create more problems and think we're doing God a favor. Sometimes we just have to remember that it is God's grace and Spirit that draws sinners. Jesus said, "And I, if I am lifted up from the earth, will draw all *peoples* to Myself" (John 12:32).

Of course, God anoints and appoints us. We are messengers of the Gospel, as I explained in the prior chapter. But the whole point of this chapter is for us to view ministry as God sees it…a beautiful mess. I'm weary of seeing young adults stressing themselves out trying to be bigger and brighter. I'm tired of seeing people call it quits after messing up or falling short. It breaks my heart to see God's children trying to outdo each other and generate more "Likes" on Facebook. All of this church posturing and upstaging needs to stop.

Psalm 100:2 says, "Serve the LORD with gladness; come before His presence with singing". Don't minister chiefly because of your passion to minister or your passion for your cause. Do it because you love Jesus and for the joy of serving Him alone. Do it for His glory and fame. Don't allow your gifts, your talents, your ministry, your family pedigree, your title, your ideas, your trophies or your image to become your idols.

We are called to love the Caller, not the calling; the Dream-giver, not the dream.

Perfectly Broken

Light can only shine through broken vessels. And since we're made of clay, not glass, brokenness is the secret to releasing what God has ignited in you. Of course, there's nothing appealing about a broken vessel. If something breaks in a store, it's pulled off the shelf and thrown away. But in God's store, nothing is useful *until* it's broken.

In Psalm 51:17, King David penned these words: "The sacrifices of God are a broken spirit; a broken and contrite heart—These, O God, you will not despise."

I have read this verse numerous times. And I'll be honest.

At times I've loved it. At times I haven't.

I loved this scripture whenever I felt broken or hurt. It medicated me. It put my brokenness in context. But I didn't love this scripture when things were going smooth and basically felt unbroken. I tended to shut out Psalm 51:17 when things were going good. Somehow, I believed that God wanted me "broken", which I defined as being distressed or remorseful. But a proper reading of the scripture debunks that theory.

I've learned that this scripture is not portraying a sadistic God who enjoys our pain. Also, it does not contradict the abundant life that Jesus promises in John 10:10.

Brokenness is less literal and more spiritual. God isn't saying, "I'm drawn to all broken things". You can be broken, and not repentant; sorry you got caught, but not humbled. You can be wounded and still be unforgiving and vicious. Sometimes we glorify brokenness as a stamp of piety. But notice the scripture says, "The sacrifices of God are a broken *spirit…*" God is attracted to spiritual brokenness.

Yes, God allows us to be physically, emotionally or financially broken. All of God's children will experience His chastisement and tough love, but it's always with the intent of shaping our spirit or proving our faith in Christ.

David wrote Psalm 51 in the aftermath of his affair with Bathsheba. You can feel his sorrow pulsating on the pages.

There are other examples in scripture of men who remained unbrokenly broken—a beautiful mess.

Look again at the apostle Paul who once vented about his "thorn in the flesh". There are different views on what exactly Paul's thorn was. Whatever it was, it wasn't pleasant or else Paul wouldn't have prayed three times for it to depart. It had to be either painful or irritating.

What interests me is what came as a result of Paul's thorn:

1. Humility

Paul stated, "...a thorn in the flesh was given to me, a messenger of Satan to buffet me, lest I be exalted above measure" (2 Cor. 12:7). He understood that his thorn produced humility. When you're gifted or effective, there's always a risk of "being exalted above measure", or becoming arrogant. God will, of course, exalt the humble (Ref. 1 Peter 5:6). But Paul's choice of the words, "above measure" denotes an elevated status among other believers.

Perfectly broken people are not immune from arrogance, but certainly better protected.

2. Grace

God's answer to Paul's prayer was, "My grace is sufficient for you, for My strength is made perfect in weakness..." (2 Cor. 12:9). What makes the mess so beautiful? How is it possible for God to use imperfect, broken people? Grace.

All forms of ministry are displays of God's grace working through the weakness (mess) of men and women. We serve both *from* and *through* God's sufficient grace. His strength, not ours, does all the heavy lifting.

Perfect strength, through grace, manifests in our weakness for God's own purpose and glory. Until we unlock the meaning of grace in our lives, we'll continue to base our ministry success on human efforts instead of God's divine ability to draw men unto Himself. As recipients of His lavish grace, our delight is that He chooses us, includes us and ultimately cares for us.

3. Power

Paul's thought continues, "…Therefore most gladly I will rather boast in my infirmities, that the power of Christ may rest upon me" (2 Cor. 12:9). Paul did what we rarely do, especially those in public ministry. He boasted *in* his infirmities. He showed his battle scars, so to speak. But that vulnerability, that level of honesty gave God an avenue to release His power.

God's power is not channeled through the veins of human power. He doesn't need us to be strong. We must have Paul's disposition, "…For when I am weak, then I am strong" (2 Cor. 12:10). All power flows from God and is meant for His glory. Whatever talent, anointing or gift you have, God gave it to you freely by His grace.

This might be the most un-ministry chapter on ministry you've ever read. I'm okay with that. This wasn't really about what you do, but who you are.

I end this chapter the way it began, except I'm not that 12-year-old kid anymore. I've grown up. And now my mistakes and weaknesses are magnified. I've got children who look up to me and a church who sees me as their leader. As you get older, the stakes are higher. I'm not trying to scare you, either. I simply urge you to discover God's grace in serving and ministering. Allow God to cover you and flow through your perceived weaknesses.

Here's the reality. You're going to fail at some point. You're going to come face to face with your flaws. You will probably handle certain situations wrong. In other words, you're going to blow it at some point. And if you sin, you still need to repent, but don't live your life as if every blemish, failure or weakness is a sign that you're not qualified for God's mission.

Actually, it's a sign that you're human.

Shift Keys

1. Accept your weaknesses – If you find yourself under constant pressure to polish your image, it's time to stop. Your weaknesses are portals of grace. By accepting your weaknesses, you can better identify with those who feel inadequate. Also, it defuses the urge to outperform others and exaggerate your successes.

2. Love the Caller – Unfortunately we rarely confront our "Christian idols". Those are the things *of* God we substitute *for* God. This happens subtly and is easily masked. Think of what your intimacy with God would be like without *any* official ministry or cause. Would you pray if you didn't preach? Love the Caller before the calling. Love people, not the system or brand.

2. Get to work – Human messiness and weakness is not an excuse to do nothing. God's grace is not for us to slack in our service and labor. Don't sit back and think, "God will do it", but get up and say, "God will do it…*through* me". You're the instrument God wants to use to manifest His love and grace in the world.

11 | Vintage Faith

Generation to Generation

Americans are fascinated with vintage stuff: cars, clothes, art, tin cans, décor, instruments, toys and a plethora of rare items you can usually find on eBay. Personally, I'm drawn to vintage books. There's something magical about leafing through the musty pages of an old book. It's like stepping into a time machine and being transported to another era.

Vintage represents something that's old but not outdated, historic but not irrelevant. Anything that's vintage is timeless and worth saving or passing along. I would like to borrow this term and humbly suggest that our Apostolic faith is vintage—classic, authentic and worth preserving.

Just because something is vintage doesn't guarantee its going be treasured. If not honored or treated with care, it can rust or be auctioned off. The apostle Paul reminded young Timothy of his vintage faith and Godly heritage: "When I call to remembrance the genuine faith that is in you, which dwelt first in your grandmother Lois and your mother Eunice, and I am persuaded is in you also" (2 Timothy 1:5).

Timothy was reminded that his genuine faith did not originate with himself, but with his grandmother Lois. He was walking in a dimension of faith and blessing that began two generations before him. His mother Eunice played an active role in handing down her beliefs and values. She didn't just assume that because Timothy grew up in a Christian home that he would automatically cling to their faith.

Paul must have been close to the family because he had personal insight about Timothy's heritage. Therefore, he felt confident that Timothy would carry the legacy and *own* his faith.

Notice the adjective Paul uses before the word "faith". He writes: "I call to remembrance the *genuine* faith…" The word for "genuine" literally means "without playing the part". Paul was proud of Timothy for staying true, for not watering down his beliefs in an age of hypocrisy, worldliness and twisted theology.

One could assume, "Of course Timothy was a faithful Christian. He grew up in a sheltered environment. His whole family was probably supportive and encouraging". Here is the reality of Timothy's upbringing:

- His father was a Greek (Acts 16:3) and did not share his wife's Jewish beliefs. This would have created tension in the house and possibly made it easier for Timothy to choose an ungodly lifestyle.

- Perhaps because his father was a Greek, we only read of Timothy's mother, Eunice who taught him to serve and love Jesus (1 Timothy 1:5). The odds were certainly against him.

- According to some scholars, Lystra (Timothy's hometown) did not have a Jewish synagogue. It's not likely that Timothy "slept under the pews", so to speak. Therefore, he didn't have any synagogue training and certainly no Sunday School.

Timothy's faith did not come automatically. It took dedication from his mother and a willingness from him to learn and be convinced. His heritage was not a religious institution or mere tradition. But rather, it was a fusion of faith and God's Word.

Later in his letter, Paul writes: "But you must remain faithful to the things you have been taught. You know they are true, for you know you can trust those who taught you. You have been taught the holy Scriptures from childhood, and they have given you the wisdom to receive the salvation that comes by trusting in Christ Jesus" (2 Timothy 3:14-15, NLT).

Let's explore two key ideas from this scripture.

1. Truth

Paul urged Timothy to remain faithful to the truth. In other words, don't allow other false doctrines, theories and philosophies to pollute the pure Apostolic doctrine of Jesus Christ. As a young adult, don't allow some new or trendy doctrine change your mind. Don't allow men to thwart the truth by citing creeds and theologians instead of the Scripture alone. Don't be wooed away by crafty talk, intellectualism or false piety. Tighten your grip on your faith. Own it!

Paul wrote: "For the time will come when people will not put up with sound doctrine. Instead, to suit their own desires, they will gather around them a great number of teachers to say what their itching ears want to hear" (2 Timothy 4:3, NIV). Isn't it obvious that people are being led astray today? I'm not talking about new believers or first generation believers. I'm talking about second, third and fourth generation young adults abandoning the truth they were taught as children.

As an Apostolic follower of Jesus, you must be assured of what you believe. You must pursue an intimate relationship with Jesus and deepen your understanding of the Scriptures. If not, an astute speaker, a liberal thinker, an agnostic or even an atheist could confuse you. Don't base your theology or beliefs on clichés, one-liners and sermon titles. Don't rely solely on your parent's knowledge or pastor's teachings.

Explore the Apostolic theology and sharpen your knowledge on essential doctrines such as the Oneness of God, water baptism in The Name of Jesus Christ and also the baptism of the Holy Spirit. Read the Gospel narratives again— Matthew, Mark, Luke and John. Let your heart be truly gospeled, not just indoctrinated. Seek to better understand why Jesus died on the Cross, was buried and rose three days later.

2. Trust

Paul said to Timothy, "You know you can trust those who taught you". Paul isn't just making a doctrinal appeal, but a relational appeal. He wanted to replay the video of Timothy's upbringing, possibly to remind him that he could trust the teachings, because he could trust the ones who taught him.

It's all about relationship.

The people who taught Timothy were not strangers. He had personal relationships with his teachers, namely Eunice (his mother) and Lois (his grandmother). They were authority figures in his life, people he could count on.

Anytime there is an element of trust, there is always the potential of mistrust. I've observed that in some cases, young adults will abandon their faith because someone in church authority mistreated them. It could leave him or her feeling soured or disenchanted. As the wound festers it can harden the heart or kindle cynicism towards the Church and even its doctrine.

It's tough to persuade a wounded person to come home because his or her reasons for leaving are, in many cases, rational. Unfortunately, they have experienced the messy side of an imperfect community. However, I'm hopeful that those who have been wounded by a church experience, maybe you, can find your way home through forgiveness and healing.

The words "You know you can trust those who taught you" must have evoked memories and emotions as Timothy pictured his mother praying by his bedside. Maybe he heard the echo of her voice reciting Hebrew Scriptures or singing old hymns. Paul wanted Timothy to associate *truth* with *trusted* people in his life. He wanted to assure him that those who poured into him, loved him and prayed for him wanted the best for him. In other words, truth is personal.

Dropped Calls

The relationship between past and emerging generations is fragile. As a younger believer, a variety of problems and pressures could derail your faith. But to be honest, it's not entirely your responsibility. As a boy, Samuel slept in the temple, but he didn't know the Lord (Ref. 1 Samuel 3:1-10).

The irony is undeniable.

Samuel was not only a church kid, but more like a pastor's kid. Under the guardianship of the priest Eli, Samuel was immersed in the religious subculture and spent the majority of his time serving in the temple. Yet in spite of his disciplines and godly environment, he didn't know the Lord for himself. It would seem that if anybody knew the Lord, it would be Samuel.

After all, he slept in the sanctuary!

Before we criticize him, let's cut Samuel some slack. We can't blame him for not initially recognizing God's voice. He had never heard it before. This was a new experience for him, one that would catapult his prophetic ministry. Had it not been for Eli, who coached Samuel on how to respond to God's call, the call might have been dropped all together.

In her book, *Almost Christian*, Kenda Creasy Dean asserts: "We "teach" young people baseball, but we "expose" them to faith. We provide coaching and opportunities for youth to develop and improve their pitches and their SAT scores, but we blithely assume that religious identity will happen by osmosis, emerging "when youth are ready" (a confidence we generally lack when it comes to, say, algebra)."[12]

Transferring a legacy from one generation to the next can be a delicate process—as delicate as carrying and transferring an egg with just spoons. It requires focus on both sides.

The teacher must be willing to teach.

The learner must be willing to learn.

Unfortunately, Eli wasn't as consistent with his own sons. Instead of rebuking them for polluting the temple with immoral behavior such as theft and fornication, he swept it under the rug. In yet another twist of irony, Samuel's first prophetic word spelled out doom for Eli. He and his two sons ended up paying a high price for his negligence.

There are also examples in Scripture where the blame falls mostly, if not entirely on the next generation. When King Saul disobeyed God's instructions to obliterate the Amalekites by sparing the king and his treasures, he found himself at odds with God (Ref. 1 Samuel 13:5-14). Samuel, who was now an elderly priest, had personally anointed Saul as Israel's first king. But as the years went by, he witnessed Saul slip further into rebellion. Saul's arrogance polluted his anointing and cast a dark shadow over the throne.

The call was dropped.

As a fifth generation believer, I have a rich heritage of faith

---

[12] Dean, Kenda Creasy (2010-06-12). Almost Christian : What the Faith of Our Teenagers is Telling the American Church (p. 15). Oxford University Press. Kindle Edition.

in Jesus Christ. I've got vintage faith and trust me, I'm proud of it. I'm standing on the shoulders of my forefather's prayers and God's faithfulness. I'm blessed, perhaps like you, to have been handed His glorious gospel and legacy of Apostolic ministry. It's not something I take for granted.

However, I've come to realize that heritage only gives you some track shoes and a course to run on. It's up to us to lace up and run the race. I won't catch the baton if I'm sitting in the bleachers of complacency or running on the opposite track of self-righteousness. There comes a point in every young believer's life where they have to decide who they're going to be.

Collide vs. Collaborate

The dichotomy between the wisdom of the older generation and the zeal of the newer generation presents us with two options: collide or collaborate. If we collide, we may find ourselves stalemated, deadlocked in a church debate where everybody loses. No organization, church or business is immune from silos in which barriers can develop and stunt its long-term growth.

So long as we're not tampering with our essential doctrines, it seems reasonable to adopt or enrich a collaborative culture. But since I'm still a younger believer myself, I'm compelled to awaken my generation and remind them that we must be willing to listen before demanding a voice.

Many times we react to old models and conclusions from one side of the spectrum. We often try to reform without understanding the original form—why things are the way they are and the historical forces that influenced those paradigms. This is true in nearly all forms of tradition, such as church, family and culture.

In a society that shuns tradition but idolizes youthfulness and modernism, you should study history before having an estate sale on everything that seems old and out-of-date.

Some of our traditions are vintage, enduring values that should appreciate over time, like classic baseball cards. Not everything old is outdated. Not everything new is necessary. I've listened to some of my peers who criticize our tradition without any historical and sociological context. Some are even willing to disassociate from Spirit-led denominations over what they feel is a lack of change or response to current trends.

If our generation isn't careful, it could cast its own mold of cultural blindness even while criticizing it in the previous generation. In others words, you'll soon find yourself as narrow-minded as those you disagree with. I'm not suggesting that we accept all forms of tradition and deny ourselves of progress.

Churches that don't adapt will fossilize and become museums of what God *did,* instead of what He's *doing.*

The key to a generational shift is to temper our zeal with patience. Jesus waited until he was publicly endorsed by John the Baptist (prior generation) before launching His public ministry — which would shift the foundation of religion. At twelve-years-old, Jesus interpreted scriptures to the scholars and was about his Father's business. But not until He was thirty-years-old, was He poised to interpret the times and catalyze change.

Jesus honored the stages of human and social development. He let His message cook in His heart until it was the right time. This serves to remind us that the right idea, at the wrong time, is the wrong idea.

Yesterday's prophets are today's historians. The older generation in the Church knows that change will happen and in many cases, they were the reformers of their time. As young believers, ministers and pastors, we need to run our race with patience and take advantage of those wise mentors who surround us.

In order to facilitate change within the Church, we need intergenerational relationships. These relationships are the keys to preserving essentials like doctrine and theology while reforming nonessentials like practices and methods.

Father, May I?

As kids, many of us used to play the game, "Mother, may I?" One kid would play the role of mother and would stand at one end of the room while all the other children would line up at the other end. The children would take turns asking questions like, "Mother, may I take three giant steps forward?" Or "Mother, may I take ten baby steps forward?" The mother could reply, "Yes, you may" or "No, you may not, but you may (blank) instead". I used to love playing the role of mother for the obvious reasons – I got to be in charge!

By exchanging the title "mother" with "father", this child's game reminds me of how important it is for you to be spiritually fathered.

Too many young adults fall into trouble and even heresy because they haven't allowed themselves to be "fathered". Clouded by their gifts, education or ambition, they refuse to be corrected, and eventually argue or enlighten themselves out of God's blessing. The apostle Paul diagnosed this problem in his letter to the Corinthians: "For though you might have ten thousand instructors in Christ, yet *you do not have* many fathers; for in Christ Jesus I have begotten you through the Gospel. Therefore I urge you, imitate me" (1 Cor. 4:15-16).

God is a God of generations. That's His chosen channel to release spiritual blessings and authority. During a sermon at

Solomon's porch, Peter alluded to this reality: "The God of Abraham, Isaac, and Jacob, the God of our fathers, glorified His Servant Jesus…" (Acts 3:13). Furthermore, Jesus is given two unique titles: the Son of Man and the Son of God. "Son of" denotes generational order and identity.

If you claim to be a child of God, great! That's your Gospel identity as a born-again Christian. But the question is, who is fathering you? Paul didn't say, "…I urge you, imitate *Jesus*." Instead he emphasizes spiritual fathering and said, "Imitate *me*".

The concept of generational blessing and cursing is woven into the Biblical narrative. A negative example is when Noah cursed his son Ham for not covering his nakedness. Even though Noah was morally wrong, being plastered with wine, his curse against Ham and his posterity was final. Noah's other two sons, Shem and Japheth, walked backwards into their father's tent and covered his shame (Ref. Genesis 9).

Ham was right in one sense, but wrong in the greater sense. He was truthful to his brothers. Their dad *was* drunk and naked. He had good reason to be critical. But his error came in how he handled the incident. Instead of protecting Noah's honor, he scandalized him.

Here's the point: even if you disagree with your elders, take your cues from Shem and Japheth, who guarded their relationship with honor.

Let's briefly look at the older generation's responsibility.

When God instructed Abraham to build an altar and sacrifice his son Isaac, who was physically stronger, the younger generation submitted against human logic. The key to Isaac's survival, however, was Abraham's ability to hear God's voice (Ref. Genesis 22). God spoke to Abraham, not to Isaac.

Because this father-son relationship was authentic, Isaac surrendered total control of his future. He could have fled or resisted with physical force at any point. He simply listened to his father.

As Isaac listened to his father, his father Abraham listened to his Heavenly Father.

If you're in Abraham's position, then you have a great responsibility to know God's voice. Elder leaders who become deaf to God's voice will sacrifice tomorrow's leaders on the altar of yesterday's revelation. But if you're attuned to God's voice, you will see the ram in the thorn bush (the crucified Christ) whose grace covers all generations.

Young adults, we need mentors who will disciple us, lest our testimony resemble Joshua 2:10 which reads, "When all that generation had been gathered to their fathers, another generation arose after them who did not know the Lord nor the work which He had done for Israel." This text is a wake-up call. It reminds us how fragile a shift can be.

But it shouldn't frighten us.

I believe that if we engage in healthy dialogue and enrich our relationships, God will grant us the grace to move forward. Your best days are ahead of you. You are chosen by God for this hour. Make the shifts that you need to make – upward shifts, inward shifts and forward shifts.

Now is the time to shift and allow God's purpose to prevail in your life. Be the Apostolic young adult that God has called you to be.

Shift Keys

1. Engage truth – Become a student of Scripture, not just theory and philosophy. Don't let experiences shape your theology. Rather, let theology shape your experiences. Let Scripture speak for itself. Guard your heart from subtle forms of humanism and moral relativism.

2. Value your faith – There's going to come a day when you want to pass something down to your children. Make sure you have something to give them. Value your faith and the blood, sweat and tears it took to preserve it over the years. Cherish the Gospel of Jesus Christ, the Apostolic doctrine and the heritage of the faith. This doesn't mean that our Church won't evolve to changing times, but our core beliefs are timeless.

3. Listen to counsel – Listen to the counsel of your spiritual fathers. The wisest man in scripture, King Solomon, wrote the following, "Listen to advice and accept instruction, and in the end you will be wise" (Proverbs 19:20 NIV). Evaluate the relationships in your life and identify your sources of counsel. Perhaps you're missing a spiritual mentor, as this will make a world of difference in your spiritual development.

Conclusion

As I conclude this book, I am reminded of why I wrote it in the first place: because I have been where you are. Of course our stories are different, but I remember being in my early 20's and wondering "now what?" Every chapter in this book is a reflection of my own journey, in one way or another.

I chose not to inflate this book with untested platitudes or hyperbole, simply to boost my popularity or book sales. What we desire is an unscripted discussion – not just advice, but affirmation – someone to say "I understand and here's what I've learned". In that regard, it's okay to ask questions, to make mistakes, to face insecurities and admit we don't always know what do to.

Sometimes as young adults we feel like giving up on our dreams after one bad decision or misfortune. We don't realize that in the trajectory of our lives, we're going to make repeated mistakes and find ourselves in difficult circumstances. Never take advice from someone who doesn't have regrets or admit their failures, because chances are they're either dishonest or blind to their own humanity. I'm not perfect. Neither are you. We are here by God's grace and through that grace we can shift into the next season of our lives.

One thing is for sure; this conversation is not over. In fact it's just the beginning—in your small group, around the dinner table, on Facebook and Twitter, and anywhere else you gather. If this book has changed your life or helped you in any way, recommend it to someone. Maybe you didn't always agree with my advice. If so, that's okay. Talk it over in your discussion group or with a mentor. Study or meditate on the Scriptures in this book. Get familiar with your Bible (not the App, but the printed version).

Finally, I pray that God would grant you favor and genuine success in your faith, life and mission. I pray that you find direction and discover the ultimate joy of being a follower of Jesus Christ. You are an Apostolic young adult, full of power and possibility. Let your light shine. Become who God has created you to be.

About the Author

JACOB RODRIGUEZ is an author and pastor. Jacob has authored multiple books which include, *The Lord's Lady* and *Crave*. He has a passion to reach people with the Gospel and expand the Kingdom of God.

Jacob and his wife, Cherie, reside in the Silicon Valley with their two young children, Makai and Chloe.

To learn more, visit the following websites:

- www.jacobrodriguez.org

- www.citylightonline.org

Made in the USA
Charleston, SC
25 July 2013